COARSE ACTING STRIKES BACK

Four More Coarse plays

by Michael Green

SAMUEL FRENCH

samuelfrench.co.uk

FOR AMATEUR PRODUCTION ENQUIRIES

UNITED KINGDOM AND WORLD
EXCLUDING NORTH AMERICA
plays@samuelfrench.co.uk
020 7255 4302/01

Each title is subject to availability from Samuel French,
depending upon country of performance.

THINKING ABOUT PERFORMING A SHOW?

There are thousands of plays and musicals available to perform from Samuel French right now, and applying for a licence is easier and more affordable than you might think

From classic plays to brand new musicals, from monologues to epic dramas, there are shows for everyone.

Plays and musicals are protected by copyright law, so if you want to perform them, the first thing you'll need is a licence. This simple process helps support the playwright by ensuring they get paid for their work and means that you'll have the documents you need to stage the show in public.

Not all our shows are available to perform all the time, so it's important to check and apply for a licence before you start rehearsals or commit to doing the show.

LEARN MORE & FIND THOUSANDS OF SHOWS

Browse our full range of plays and musicals, and find out more about how to license a show
www.samuelfrench.co.uk/perform

Talk to the friendly experts in our Licensing team for advice on choosing a show and help with licensing
plays@samuelfrench.co.uk   020 7387 9373

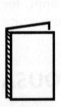 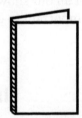

**Other plays by MICHAEL GREEN
published and licensed by Samuel French**

Four Plays for Coarse Actors
Streuth
I Fornicazione
A Collier's Tuesday Tea
All's Well That Ends As You Like It

The Coarse Acting Show 2
Moby Dick
The Cherry Sisters
Last Call for Breakfast
Henry the Tenth (Part Seven)

The Third Great Coarse Acting Show
A Fish in Her Kettle by David Pearson
Present Slaughter by Jane Dewey and Don Starkey
The Vagabond Prince by Simon Brett with music and lyrics
by John Gould
Stalag 69 by Michael Green
Julius and Cleopatra by Michael Green

Umlaut Prince of Düsseldorf

Haggard – An Entertainment by Eric Chappell based on
characters created by Michael Green

**Other titles by MICHAEL GREEN
published by Samuel French**

The Art of Coarse Acting

**FIND PERFECT PLAYS TO PERFORM AT
www.samuelfrench.co.uk/perform**

MUSIC USE NOTE

Licensees are solely responsible for obtaining formal written permission from copyright owners to use copyrighted music in the performance of this play and are strongly cautioned to do so. If no such permission is obtained by the licensee, then the licensee must use only original music that the licensee owns and controls. Licensees are solely responsible and liable for all music clearances and shall indemnify the copyright owners of the play(s) and their licensing agent, Samuel French, against any costs, expenses, losses and liabilities arising from the use of music by licensees. Please contact the appropriate music licensing authority in your territory for the rights to any incidental music.

USE OF COPYRIGHT MUSIC

A licence issued by Samuel French Ltd to perform this play does not include permission to use the incidental music specified in this copy. Where the place of performance is already licensed by the PERFORMING RIGHT SOCIETY (PRS) a return of the music used must be made to them. If the place of performance is not so licensed then application should be made to the PRS, 2 Pancras Square, London, N1C 4AG. A separate and additional licence from PHONOGRAPHIC PERFORMANCE LTD, 1 Upper James Street, London W1F 9DE (www.ppluk.com) is needed whenever commercial recordings are used.

IMPORTANT BILLING AND CREDIT REQUIREMENTS

If you have obtained performance rights to this title, please refer to your licensing agreement for important billing and credit requirements.

ABOUT THE AUTHOR

Michael Green was born in Leicester, England in 1927 and started writing as a reporter on the local newspaper. He has never been a lumberjack or sold hot dogs. Since publication in 1960 of his first book, *The Art of Coarse Rugby*, he has been a full-time author specialising in telling the grim truth about such pursuits as golf, sailing, drinking, moving and acting, and his books have sold over a million copies world-wide. In 1977 he took a company of amateurs to The Edinburgh Festival with a stage version of The Art of Coarse Acting called *The Coarse Acting Show*, and it was hailed as the comedy hit of the season. Two years later, *The Coarse Acting Show 2* was awarded a "Fringe First" at The Edinburgh Festival and then transferred to London's West End for three months. But Michael remains modest. "I have a great deal to be modest about", he says. He died in February 2018, aged 91.

INTRODUCTION

This fourth volume of Coarse plays actually has more parts for women than men (loud cheers). Men had the best of things in the earlier plays, partly because some were pastiches of classic drama such as Shakespeare, and I am delighted the balance is restored. But if any of the pieces printed here are still not suitable, it would be possible to substitute a play from the earlier volumes and have a mixture. In that case a useful blanket title is *The Coarse Acting Show,* although strictly that is the sub-title of volume one *(Four Plays for Coarse Actors).*

Introducing a fourth volume of these plays is rather like inviting an actor to a party–you think everybody will know who they are, and then you find they don't. I hope most readers will know what Coarse Acting is, either from my book *The Art of Coarse Acting* or from the other three volumes of plays. However, one can't be sure, so once again, here's a brief explanation of what it's all about, with apologies to those who've read it all before.

In *The Art of Coarse Acting,* on which the plays are based, I give several definitions of a Coarse Actor (I use the word to include the female). The original was "one who could remember the lines but not the order in which they come", but as the years passed further definitions thrust themselves into my experience and sometimes into my face. For instance, a performance at the Edinburgh Festival Fringe suggested a Coarse Actor was one who limps on both legs simultaneously, while an unfortunate incident in another play indicated him as one who knows when to come on stage but not where. Then there was the woman I played with who knew the last play better than the one she was actually in.

So definitions can be extended indefinitely (I later acted with a chap who knew the next play better than the one he was actually in). But there is more to it than just incompetence. Coarse Acting covers every kind of misplaced performance from people who do imitations of Laurence Olivier to frightened players in their first part. Cliché performances are popular, in which all colonels have blood pressure and all cleaners Cockney accents. Frequently the character is based on something seen on film or TV. Some Coarse Actors are accident-prone while many have a compulsion to overdo it, so they play every part with a limp, something that is popular in crowd scenes, or else have an outrageous accent. Age doesn't mean maturity, it means senility. But one feature common to all is that they think every performance was a success. "Believe me, old chap, the audience never noticed anything wrong," is the Coarse Actor's battle-cry. Over-confidence is their trademark.

Then there's Coarse stage management, brought to the audience's attention by a jammed door, a candle that won't light or a gun which won't fire. There's Coarse lighting, sound and wardrobe, and even directing, which may result in the whole cast finishing up huddled in one corner of the set. In fact, the acting can be fine but what goes on around the cast can still turn the show into Coarse Theatre.

This series of plays began as the result of a Coarse Acting competition at The Questors Theatre, Ealing, way back in 1972, in which various teams competed to see who could produce the funniest portrayal of stage disaster. People enjoyed the playlets so much other contests were held, competitors including teams from The Royal Shakespeare Company and the National Theatre. Later, some of the best plays were put together in one show and after a successful run at the Edinburgh Fringe, the first volume was published. To be followed by the second, which transferred from the Edinburgh Fringe to the Shaftesbury Theatre, London...and the third...and now the fourth.

Basically, they are simply spoofs on bad amateur dramatics, or bad professional dramatics if you like. A send-up. And the plays themselves are pastiches of different types of drama. But like all send-ups, they rely on a basis of truth. The cast are trying to put on a successful show. They aren't all rotten actors and actresses. It's just that everything keeps going wrong...

The contrast between the earnest efforts of the cast and the disasters that befall them is an essential part of the humour. If all the cast are way over the top then the show won't be funny. Which is why the best actors and actresses do so well in the Coarse plays, because they can successfully parody types of actor and styles of drama. Genuine Coarse Actors are hopeless in a Coarse Acting play.

Directing requires an idea of the original which is being parodied, plus good comic instinct. Nothing is less amusing than a bad Coarse Acting play. I know. I've seen some. A few failed because the cast couldn't act; some because they'd ignored the stage directions (not to mention the script); others because the director had approached from the wrong angle.

The plays also require discipline. Strange how they bring out the worst in people. Usually the first rehearsal is like something out of an 18th century lunatic asylum, with everybody gibbering and foaming at each other. In directing I found it useful to have a rehearsal at which the play was performed straight. This proved effective in bringing the cast back to earth. The danger period is halfway through rehearsals when the lines have stopped being funny and the cast start trying to make everybody laugh again. There's a similar danger spot during the run, when over-confidence takes over.

Having issued these warnings, I'm pleased to say most shows were very amusing indeed. Some companies introduced ideas of their own and this is welcome, the sole criterion being that they work. A few innovations were so good I incorporated them in revised editions. Others were so bad I tried to forget them, especially the company who changed the ending of one piece because they didn't want to pay for a particular prop. I was impressed by the casts' different interpretations of parts, but tampering with the lines rarely worked.

If this sounds rather earnest, I can only say comedy is a serious business. It's the audience who need to laugh, not the actors. Notwithstanding that, have fun and good luck. I'd say "break a leg", but I really did once when I fell off the stage, and it wasn't very pleasant. Apart from anything else they carried me to hospital dressed as an 18th century pirate, complete with eye-patch and wooden leg. The doctor was not amused but the stage manager was in fits.

As regards the running order, it is recommended that *Trapped* should start because sometimes an audience needs introducing to Coarse Acting. Alas, they don't always realise the show is a send-up and have been heard to say, "It was awful. Things kept going wrong." Hopefully, *Trapped* should make the point and the rather extensive set can be put up before the show. Try to let people know what to expect through publicity and the programme. The gaps between plays can be a problem. One company actually served a three-course meal (a course between each play) and another introduced a Coarse pianist, who kept losing his music. In the revised version of the first volume *(Four Plays for Coarse Actors)* I wrote in a Vicar, who made announcements between plays, such as a hospital bulletin on the lighting man, who was electrocuted during rehearsal. But experience has shown the audience are quite happy to chat and look at their programmes.

Michael Green,
2000

TRAPPED

TRAPPED

By Michael Green

First performed at The Questors Theatre, Ealing, London, on 11th April, 1996, as part of "Coarse Acting–The Revenge", with the following cast:

HOUSE MANAGER	Ossie Peled
MAID	Janet Egan
MAJOR THOMPSON	Mark Redrup
MRS THOMPSON	Lesley White
COUSIN FREDA	Pam Gower
COUSIN SHEILA	Ann Harries
BRAITHWAITE	Keith Parry
COUSIN GEORGE	John Kearns
POLICEMAN (STAGE MANAGER)	Mari King

Directed by **Michael Green**

PRODUCTION NOTES

Trapped is a pastiche of the country-house stage thriller. These all seem to be fixed in a vague period in the past, as if the clock stopped in 1949; so the show will need flats painted to represent a country house and plenty of tweeds, together with appropriate props (such as a silver tankard or a grandfather clock). Don't over-exaggerate the acting–the characters are ludicrous enough already and they must be believable.

It is important that the setting should be solid. After all, it is supposed to be a play about a group of people who can't get out of a room. However, if a full box set is really impossible, flats could be used for the doors and furniture placed in the gaps, thus partly sustaining the illusion at any rate. The french windows are never opened, so it's easy to make them come adrift when the Major attacks them. As regards the other two doors, one swings open; it's vital it doesn't do this before it has to. The other falls off under the Major's assault. In the original production this was achieved by replacing the hinge-pins by long nails with a nylon thread attached. These were pulled out from backstage at the appropriate time. But other methods may prove suitable. If necessary, it is possible to do the play with only one door besides the french windows, cutting out references to the second one. In that case, the door needn't collapse. But two is more fun.

Although the door of the built-in cupboard doesn't open it must be practical, so it can rattle and shake when George tries to enter. A door flat could be used instead of a cupboard. Make sure the audience has a good view of all the doors, since they are essential to the plot. Don't let furniture or the cast mask them when they come into the action. I have indicated in the script where the doors were in the original performance, but obviously a director will site them according to the needs of their own production.

Michael Green

NOTES ON THE CHARACTERS

MAJOR THOMPSON (who could well be in plus-fours) is the chief architect of disaster, which is unfortunate for him as he fancies himself in the leading role. Bought a moustache specially. Borrowed his accent from an old black-and-white war film. Alas, everything he touches goes wrong, often due to his over-enthusiasm. However, he ploughs gamely on, determined to see this ghastly business through. One suspects that offstage his biggest rival in the society is the man playing the villain, **BRAITHWAITE**. Luckily for the major, Braithwaite is equally accident prone.

MRS THOMPSON also fancies herself as one of the company's leading lights. Her performance is rather over-intense, and based on a visit to *The Mousetrap*. She speaks in what she thinks is the voice of a rural aristocrat.

THE STAGE MANAGER who comes on as the policeman at short notice, should be played by an actress. It's an important part, but not easy, and it's necessary the comedy doesn't sag at this point.

THE HOUSE MANAGER who announces the actor's non-arrival, is also an actress's part.

COUSIN SHEILA is one of those delicate creatures who will never allow themselves to be anything but elegant on stage (even when poisoned). She has been playing all rôles in exactly the same way for thirty years and is not going to change now. Doesn't need to, as her husband runs the bank where the group have their account.

COUSIN FREDA gives what one might call a robust performance. She is more used to shouting at horses than acting.

THE MAID probably puts on a stock working-class accent, the one she used for the charlady in the last show. Unfortunately, traces of her own accent show through.

COUSIN GEORGE can't understand why he never gets large rôles. Something rotten always happens to him even in small parts. He is convinced he could have played the lead but for the prejudice of the director. Believes he saved the situation by coming through the french windows with a knife sticking out of him.

The interior of a country house.

*There are french windows diagonally left; doors right
and upstage leading to the interior of the house. Another
door right leads to a built-in cupboard. Various country-
house furnishings, including a small table laid for tea
with sandwiches etc., and a table or desk with an old-
fashioned phone. The walls have spears and shields on
them, and hopefully a stuffed animal's head–it might
be rather fun to paint it on the wall.*

Before the play begins, the **HOUSE MANAGER** *comes on
and makes the following announcement.*

HOUSE MANAGER   Ladies and gentlemen, I have an
announcement. I am afraid that Charles Worthing, who
should have played the part of the policeman, cannot appear
tonight as he has been arrested for speeding while trying
to get to the theatre. So the policeman will be read at short
notice by Annabelle Brown, the Stage Manager. She has
only had a few minutes warning of this and obviously has
had no time to familiarise herself with the details, so we
do ask your indulgence. We would also ask you, in view of
the baffling nature of this murder mystery, not to reveal
the name of the murderer when you leave the theatre, so
others may enjoy the same suspense. Thank you.

*Music (something dramatic and not quite right. Perhaps
a few bars of Beethoven's Fifth?) Slow fade of lights to
blackout, then lights up. The play begins with an empty
stage. The phone rings. Nobody comes. Eventually it
stops ringing.*

As it does so, the **MAID** *peers tentatively round the door right and then retreats. A short pause and she bursts on stage and picks up the silent phone.*

MAID   Hullo... Major Thompson's rambling and isolated old country house in Surrey.

At this point the phone starts ringing loudly. The **MAID** *is nonplussed. She looks offstage and, receiving no help, decides it's best to replace the receiver. The ringing promptly stops. She picks up the receiver and it starts again. This time it stops after a few rings.*

Hullo, Major Thompson's rambling and isolated old country house in Surrey. No, I'm afraid the major is out for the minute. *(During the rest of this speech she wanders all over the stage still holding the receiver, the wire of which proves not to be connected)* As you probably know, since he retired from the army five years ago he has devoted his life to collecting old weapons and he has one of the finest collections in the country, which is valued at many thousand of pounds and it is lucky nobody has thought of stealing them. However, he will return soon, because the family have gathered to listen to the reading of his uncle's will by the solicitor. The old man left a fortune and it would be a pity if he left it to only one member of the family because then all the others would be jealous and something nasty might occur. You're welcome. *(She realises she is twelve feet from the phone and trying to pretend nothing is wrong, she sidles back to it and rings off)* Ah, Major Thompson, there you are, there was a call for you. *(She looks offstage)*

Unfortunately, **MAJOR THOMPSON** *hasn't arrived yet. An alarming suspicion comes over her that she was facing the wrong door so she turns to face the upstage one and repeats the line.*

Ah, Major Thompson, there you are, there was a—

The **MAJOR** *bursts in frantically, with his wife* **MRS THOMPSON** *following, through the original door.*

The MAID *turns again.*

—a call for you.

MAJOR Thank you, Daphne. But I've more important things on my mind just now. I think it's time to read the will. The others are in the conservatory. Please call them in.

MAID Very good, sir.

The MAID *goes out through the door right.*

MAJOR *(to his wife)* Well, old girl, isn't this rather exciting? My—

He is interrupted by the return of the MAID *who has gone out through the wrong door, so she crosses the stage and exits by the upstage one.*

My three cousins, Sheila, George and Freda all coming to hear uncle's will read.

MRS THOMPSON Yes, it is rather exciting. But isn't it unfortunate that your wealthy uncle should have been a well-known eccentric all his life and is likely to have made a very peculiar will. Your relatives are also jealous of the way you have built up a world-famous collection of old weapons, and if the will is not in their favour, anything might happen, especially as the house is full of your world-famous collection of weapons.

MAJOR Anything? Like what?

MRS THOMPSON Murder, for instance.

MAJOR Steady on, old girl, you're letting your imagination run away with you.

MRS THOMPSON No, I'm not, John. There's something evil going to happen tonight, I know it, I know it. It's all too much for me. I think I'm going to...going to...going to...

At this point she is supposed to faint into his arms. Unfortunately, he has forgotten and has turned away. She turns round and totters backwards to him, hoping he will notice, but he has now started to move. She totters after him, repeating her line. Suddenly he realises, turns round swiftly, and she falls into his arms. He comforts her. Unfortunately, his moustache comes away as he kisses her.

MAJOR There, there, it'll be all right. *(He realises his moustache is missing and looks wildly for it)*

MRS THOMPSON Yes, but don't forget that the village policeman has gone down with typhoid and that a storm has just washed away the bridge over the stream on the track which leads to the road and that the only manservant has gone to visit his sick aunt, so that we are completely isolated.

MAJOR Don't worry, old girl. There's always the telephone. *(He finds his moustache. Ideally, it should be stuck to his wife's face. He turns away and sticks it back on the slant, or upside down)*

MRS THOMPSON Of course. How silly of me. *(She picks up the receiver)* That's funny. It's gone dead.

MAJOR Probably the bally old exchange again. It'll be all right, I tell you.

*The **MAID** enters upstage.*

MAID Mr Braithwaite, Cousin Freda and Cousin Sheila.

*They enter. **BRAITHWAITE** is in a dark suit, and carrying a briefcase. The cousins are middle-aged or elderly. **COUSIN FREDA** might be in riding kit.*

*The **MAID** exits.*

MAJOR Ah, come in, everybody. Don't think you've met my wife, Alice. My dear, this is Mr Braithwaite, from uncle's solicitors, and this is Cousin Freda and Cousin Sheila. Where's Cousin George?

FREDA Haven't seen him since lunch.

BRAITHWAITE Well, we'll start without him. Would you all please sit down and I'll get out the will and read it.

They do so. There are not enough chairs and **FREDA** *is left standing. She forces* **MRS THOMPSON** *to yield half a seat.* **BRAITHWAITE** *takes a prominent position and starts to open his briefcase. It is locked and he has lost the key. He tries to force it to no avail. Desperate, he seizes a knife from the tea table and tries to prise it open. Finally he bangs it on the floor and then kicks it. No luck. He gives up.*

Well–er–I'm sure you don't want to hear me reading all that rubbish about "I, being of sound mind", etc. I will just tell you the facts and you can look at the will later. Firstly, your uncle left an estate of five million pounds.

ALL Phew!

BRAITHWAITE And secondly, he left it all to Major Thompson,

Uproar, which he quells.

Well, it isn't quite as simple as that. It's all left to Major Thompson in trust and the capital is passed down on his death to the cousins–Freda, Sheila and George. So if Major Thompson should unfortunately be deceased early, you would all get a share.

FREDA It's disgraceful. I was always his favourite niece.

SHEILA And I was his god-daughter.

Sudden blackout. Confusion. Lights up. **BRAITHWAITE** *should be missing, but he couldn't find the way out in the dark and is still groping round the upstage door.*

Now that he can see, **BRAITHWAITE** *slides out.*

MAJOR Is everybody all right?

FREDA I say, where's that lawyer chap gone?

MAJOR He must have left while the lights were out.

MRS THOMPSON Why should he have done that?

MAJOR Can't say. There's no accounting for what these legal chappies do. I'll go and look for him.

> **MAJOR** *exits to look upstage. He returns to stand in the doorway, horrified, after shutting the door behind him.*

FREDA Did you find him?

MAJOR I found him all right, sprawled on the stairs. He's been murdered.

MRS THOMPSON My God.

ALL My God.

SHEILA What'll we do?

FREDA Ring the police.

MAJOR Can't. Jolly old phone's out of order. I'll go myself. *(He tries to open the upstage door, but this time he can't)* That's strange, the door won't open.

> *Sound of thunder, howling wind and storm.*

MRS THOMPSON Try the other door and the french windows.

> **MAJOR** *does so. They are firm. After the french windows he turns round dramatically.*

MAJOR That's it, then. We're trapped.

SHEILA How do you mean?

MAJOR It's no use, we're shut in this room with a homicidal maniac outside.

FREDA For God's sake try again, major.

> **MAJOR** *hammers on the upstage door, shouting.*

MAJOR Let us out, you swine, whoever you are. Let us out or it'll be the worse for you.

> *When he stops and turns away, the door swings open.*

It's no use, I tell you. It won't budge an inch. *(He goes to the french windows and tugs at them savagely)* Let us out, you inhuman fiend! *(He gets so worked up, the french windows come away in his hand. He throws the wreckage aside)* Solid as a rock! *(He tries the remaining door right)* Let us out! Will you let us out! *(Once more he is over-energetic)*

This time the door falls completely off.

Totally immoveable. It's useless. The murderous devil has blocked up our only way of escape.

The **STAGE MANAGER** *crawls to the open door and tries to pull it back with a walking stick, or even her hand. Not surprisingly, she fails.*

MRS THOMPSON Oh my God, it's so awful. *(She bursts into tears)*

MAJOR Steady on, old girl. Keep a stiff upper lip.

SHEILA I can't stand it, I tell you, I can't stand it. *(She sobs politely)*

FREDA *comforts her. The noise of the storm increases.*

MAJOR There must be a way out, there must be. *(He beats frantically at the empty space where the door fell off)* Let us out, you swine, whoever you are. *(He gives up)*

SHEILA My God, look.

MAJOR What?

SHEILA Don't you see...the cupboard door...it's slowly swinging open.

The cupboard door is doing nothing of the sort. Instead, the person inside is desperately trying to push it open, but it is jammed ("I told you that there door wouldn't fit, mate"). The handle can be seen frantically working up and down (a door knob won't be so effective) He hammers at the door from inside while the cast watch, hypnotised.

After an embarrassing pause, the **MAJOR** *tries to save the situation. Moving upstage of the cupboard door, he gives a gasp and pretends his eyes are following a body falling out. The rest pick up the cue and do the same. All stare at an imaginary spot on the carpet, while the hammering goes on inside.*

MAJOR My God, it's Cousin George.

MRS THOMPSON Is he...is he...?

The **MAJOR** *kneels by the empty space and goes through the motions of lifting an imaginary wrist and feeling a pulse. Getting no answer, he gives an imaginary kiss of life and starts pressing up and down on an imaginary chest in an effort at artificial respiration.*

MAJOR I'm afraid so, old girl.

FREDA My God, what's that sticking out of his trousers?

MAJOR Why it's the antique sword that used to hang in the hall. Stabbed through the waistband. Is there no limit to the fiend's ingenuity?

At this point **GEORGE,** *the body, having realised he is never going to get through the door, walks in through the wreckage of the french windows and carefully lies down on the carpet, complete with sword sticking out.*

(after a horrified pause) My God, it's Cousin George.

SHEILA Is he...is he...?

MAJOR *(unable to cope and a trifle hysterical)* Yes, he is...he's Cousin George... I mean he's dead...he's...he's...

FREDA *(saving the situation)* I think, major, you were going to say that it is Cousin George and he is dead and he has one of your old antique swords sticking out of his trousers and there is no limit to the fiend's ingenuity.

MAJOR Ah, yes. I was. Thank you.

MRS THOMPSON But what will we do?

FREDA Do? I'm going to have a sandwich. If we're going to be trapped here for the night we'll need some nourishment.

SHEILA Jolly good idea. I'm going to have a cup of tea.

Both of them march over to the table and serve themselves.

MRS THOMPSON What about...about...about... *(She indicates* **GEORGE***)*

MAJOR Don't worry, old girl. I'll cover him up. *(He looks round for something suitable and uses a tablecloth)*

The body is now covered, with the sword sticking obscenely out. Finding this uncomfortable, the body wriggles into a better position and adjusts the sword while the cast watch fascinated.

MRS THOMPSON Are we still trapped?

The **MAJOR** *looks in embarrassment at the wide open door upstage and goes through the motions of trying to force it open.*

MAJOR Afraid so, old girl. Solid as a rock. Oh God, is there nothing we can do?

The **MAJOR** *beats his fists on the wall in sheer frustration. They go straight through.*

FREDA *(clutching her stomach)* Aaaaah. *(She staggers around a good deal and drops dead)*

MAJOR What the devil...

SHEILA *(clutching her throat delicately)* Ahem. Ahem.

The actress playing **SHEILA** *has never got a dress dirty on stage in her life and is not going to start now. In a very well-mannered way she politely sags to the floor, making sure she has a clean spot to land on. Indeed, she may flick it clean with her handkerchief. She then expires gracefully.*

MRS THOMPSON My God, are they...are they...

MAJOR Afraid so, old girl. Looks as if the food and drink were poisoned.

SHEILA moves to make herself more comfortable and gives an apologetic smile.

MRS THOMPSON Then you and I are the only ones left.

MAJOR Looks like it, old girl.

MRS THOMPSON I can't stand it, I tell you... I can't stand any more...take me away from this horrible place...

MAJOR Steady on, old girl. I can't do that. We're trapped.

Suddenly, the upstage door is pulled to by a desperate **BRAITHWAITE**. *After a pause, it crashes open and* **BRAITHWAITE** *enters, holding a spear. Alas, he is holding it the wrong way round.*

My God, Braithwaite! So you weren't dead after all.

BRAITHWAITE No, I wasn't dead. It was all a fake. But you soon will be.

MAJOR What do you mean?

BRAITHWAITE Only you stand between me and a fortune. You see, there was a clause in the will which I didn't read out. That is, that on the death of all the cousins, I, as the family solicitor, inherit the fortune. Well, I've killed all the cousins, bar one. That leaves just you between me and the five million.

MAJOR Wait a minute...it's becoming plain. So you...

The following exchange is taken at great speed.

BRAITHWAITE Yes.

MAJOR And George?

BRAITHWAITE Exactly.

MAJOR So he...

BRAITHWAITE Yes.

MAJOR And...?

BRAITHWAITE Her too.

MAJOR But—

BRAITHWAITE Sandwiches.

MAJOR And—

BRAITHWAITE Cyanide.

MAJOR The doors?

BRAITHWAITE Keys.

MAJOR My God, you unutterable swine, you'll pay for this.

BRAITHWAITE I don't think so, major. You see, I have taken this antique spear from your collection of old weapons and tipped the point with a deadly poison, known only to students of the Orient. *(He realises the point is facing the wrong way and sheepishly turns the spear round)* One scratch will be fatal. Then with you out of the way, the money will be mine. The police will think it the work of a maniac. *(He advances upon the MAJOR threateningly, with the spear held out)*

MRS THOMPSON *(screaming)* Help!

MAJOR Don't be a fool. Don't do it, man!

BRAITHWAITE Goodbye, major. *(He raises his spear high)*

MAJOR I've still a trick in hand! You forgot about my old service revolver.

*The **MAJOR** manages to reach into a drawer. He is intended to find a revolver, but it isn't there. He frantically runs round the room trying every other drawer, cupboard or vase and muttering "My old service revolver", before eventually it is slid in from the wings. He snatches it gratefully. **BRAITHWAITE** waits frozen in the act of throwing.*

Thank God. My old service revolver! Stand back, or I fire. *(He points the pistol at* **BRAITHWAITE***)*

BRAITHWAITE *prepares to throw the spear. The* **MAJOR** *fires. There is a click.* **BRAITHWAITE** *remains frozen in the throwing position. There is another click. An embarrassed pause. Then* **BRAITHWAITE** *goes up to the* **MAJOR** *and whispers in his ear before going back to his original position, where he taps his knee significantly. The* **MAJOR** *looks at him and nods, then walks up and kicks* **BRAITHWAITE** *on the shin.* **BRAITHWAITE** *collapses.*

BRAITHWAITE *(writhing and holding his shin)* You filthy swine! The toe of your boot must have been poisoned. *(He dies as if poisoned, with much drama)*

As he does so, there is a pistol shot in the wings where the **STAGE MANAGER** *has got the emergency pistol to work. The* **MAJOR** *rushes to his wife.*

MAJOR Are you all right, old girl?

MRS THOMPSON Yes, thanks, darling, I'm better now.

There is a pause. She repeats the line.

Yes, thanks, darling, I'm better now.

There is a scuffling outside the upstage door and the **STAGE MANAGER** *enters. She is a slightly-built girl, wearing a policeman's helmet which almost covers her face and enormous boots. Otherwise she is in jeans and T-shirt. She has never acted before and is intensely nervous. The lights blind her and she peers short-sightedly through her spectacles at her script, oblivious to anything else. The script is the* **STAGE MANAGER***'s copy, in a ring binder. She reads her part in a steady gabble without punctuation or emphasis, and includes the stage directions and* **STAGE MANAGER***'s notes as part of the dialogue.*

POLICEMAN Now then what's all this about eh *he moves downstage with heavy tread and faces the assembled company* I received a report that your maid was found in a distressed condition trying to get help because there had been a murder at the hall and I would like to ask you a few questions *produces notebook and pencil from uniform pocket cue front of house.*

MAJOR That's right, officer. There have been four deaths. Here are the victims. But I thought you had typhoid.

POLICEMAN *(not looking at the victims, but reading)* I recovered this morning ha ha it is obvious something very strange has happened here. *(She stands peering at the script)*

Pause.

The **POLICEMAN** *doesn't know what happens next.*

MRS THOMPSON *(making up a line to help her)* I expect you would like to look at the bodies, wouldn't you, Constable?

Cousin **GEORGE** *obligingly pulls the cloth away from his face. The* **POLICEMAN**, *however, peers closely at her script and addresses* **MRS THOMPSON**.

POLICEMAN Oh, my God, what a terrible sight...

A spasm of pain flickers across **MRS THOMPSON**'s *face but she controls herself.*

...this is a dreadful thing to have happened in this peaceful village it all seems a completely mystery *pushes helmet on back of head and looks puzzled* perhaps you can enlighten me as to what went on sir.

MRS THOMPSON *firmly turns the* **POLICEMAN** *to face the* **MAJOR.**

MAJOR Well, superintendent, it's a long story, but the cause of all the trouble is lying there. Believe it or not, but the killer was my uncle's solicitor. *(He indicates* **BRAITHWATE***)*

POLICEMAN *(ignoring both the* **MAJOR** *and* **BRAITHWAITE,** *and instead peering at* **SHEILA***)* Oh no that is no solicitor that is well it can't be yes it is blow me down it's none other than Fraudulent Freddie the well known confidence trickster...

MRS THOMPSON *turns her to face* **BRAITHWATE.**

...he must have posed as your solicitor in order to carry out his operations shuts notebook *(she turns to* **MRS THOMPSON***)* if you don't mind sir I think you had better come down to the station and explain all this looking baffled cue lights and sound.

MRS THOMPSON *again turns the* **POLICEMAN** *towards the* **MAJOR.**

MAJOR Willingly, inspector. After all, I'm a man of leisure now *(he faces the audience and speaks the line triumphantly)* for I've just inherited five million pounds!

This is supposed to be the curtain line, but as the **STAGE MANAGER** *works the curtain, and she is on stage, nothing happens.*

Pause.

After all, I'm a man of leisure now for I've just inherited five million pounds!

The truth suddenly dawns on the **STAGE MANAGER** *and she rushes off.*

The curtain jerkily closes.

When it re-opens for the curtain call, the **STAGE MANAGER** *joins the line, and then has to run off again to close it. If there is no curtain, the same business can be carried out with blackouts.* **COUSIN GEORGE** *takes his curtain call with the knife still sticking from him.*

The End

OEDOCLES, KING OF THEBES

OEDOCLES, KING OF THEBES

By Michael Green

First performed by Richmond Shakespeare Society at The Questors Theatre, Ealing, London, on 8th October, 1995, as part of The Fourth World Coarse Acting Championships, adjudicated by Timothy West, with the following cast:

OEDOCLES	John Kipps
OVARY	Yvette Walters
AMNESIA	Marian Jardella
HYSTERECTOMY	Sheila Camfield
SCROTUM	Michael Godley
PRIESTESS	Mo Stewart
CHORUS	Heather Godley, Margaret Thompson, Joan Good, Yvette Walters, Katie Abbott, Francis Abbott
SLAVES	Simon Bargate, John Crook

Directed by **Claudette Williamson**

Note: The slaves may be played by women, or are expendable (see Production Notes). These options were not open to the director of the premiere as the parts were played by two elderly actors who refused to be cut.

PRODUCTION NOTES

Classical Greek tragedy is an art form with strong characteristics of its own. The Coarse version sends up some of these, such as the unending misery, the mutilation and the way horror is piled upon horror; together with the inevitable Chorus reciting their woeful tidings. A visit to a Greek tragedy, or at least to the local library, is recommended for those not familiar with the genre. I somehow feel Oedocles is a production by an over-ambitious group with intellectual pretensions, following a theatre trip.

The Chorus of The Women of Thebes are vital. In a genuine amateur production, they would be cast from the dregs of the acting strength, like most minor roles. Hence they are all assorted shapes, sizes and ages and rather ill-disciplined. Their leader, Hysterectomy, who only got the part because she once saw Oedipus at Stratford-on-Avon, performs with desperate sincerity, but the effect is marred by her bad breath and habit of spitting copiously as she speaks, which make fellow actors shrink away. She might lisp.

It will help if each member of the Chorus thinks up a particular character: one can be always late on stage, another moves left when the others go right, one is short-sighted, another is always two syllables behind; perhaps one is an old dear who doesn't know what's going on and another a giddy young girl. And so on.

The Chorus are largely written as speaking together, but the lines could be split among individuals.

Oedocles thinks he can act. Unfortunately, he's not as good as he thinks he is and his performance is based on something he saw on television. It consists mainly of waving his arms and clutching his head. There might be a touch of Bottom the Weaver about him. Perhaps he has a regional accent. That's one interpretation at any rate. His attendant Scrotum is an elderly actor who resents being reduced to small rôles.

Amnesia rather fancies her own glamour—her dress is cut so low her bosom is in danger of falling out. The Priestess has decided anyone mature must be an old crone so her performance is like something out of *The Hunchback of Notre Dame*.

The set can be quite simple—curtains with just a pillar or something to suggest the classical period. Rostra at the back will be useful.

Costumes should be the classic period robes or tunics. They can be made out of old sheets. Any crones in the Chorus can have garments made of dyed sacking, which is appropriate as they are a miserable lot, like all Greek choruses. Footwear is sandals, although the Chorus could be in bare feet.

Two slaves are needed to carry off the body of Ovary. They can be male or female. They are not seen to carry on the body because of the difficulty of making a stretcher that will hold a body yet collapse when needed, as it does later. If this can be overcome, it might be rather effective to have the slaves carry in the body at the beginning, especially if they got tangled up with the curtains. However, the version as written is safer and more practical and means the stretcher need only be held together with Velcro, since it never carries any weight. If having slaves is too much for cast resources they can easily be cut and the Chorus can carry off the stretcher.

Most of the longer speeches are written in blank verse, iambic pentameters, which is the rhythm Shakespeare used, and a popular metre with translators from the Greek. Make sure the stresses come in the right place because, as with all Coarse plays, the more like the real thing this is, the more successful it will be.

Finally, my thanks to Claudette Williamson and her company from Richmond Shakespeare Society, who courageously undertook the first public performance of this epic, with hilarious results.

Michael Green

Scene One

Thebes, Greece, circa 370 BC...

A bare stage, except for rostra at the back and something suggesting Ancient Greece, such as a classic column.

The lighting should suggest heat. This is an attempt at something Greek, but about 2,350 years too modern. Taverna music.

Lights up to reveal OEDOCLES, *accompanied by* SCROTUM *and* AMNESIA. *They exhibit deep woe, perhaps rather deeper than is necessary. Beside them on the floor is a stretcher, carrying a body covered in a white sheet and attended by two slaves who presumably carried it in. They can be male or female. See production notes.*

OEDOCLES O leave this precious burden on the ground,

I would with grief communicate a while.

O woe, my lovely wife she is no more.

My tears shall shower water on her grave.

AMNESIA Woe! Woe!

SCROTUM My Lord, I grieve for thee.

OEDOCLES Thanks, good Amnesia and kindly Scrotum too.
Your sympathy has touched my heart.

CHORUS OF THE WOMEN OF THEBES *enters, headed by their leader,* HYSTERECTOMY. *The* CHORUS *may be any number from three upwards. They are of assorted shapes and sizes. One could have a stick, which does dreadful execution on other people's sandalled feet. Another might*

*finish a syllable after everyone else. A third comes on
stage ten seconds late and has to surreptitiously slip into
position. Possibly one cannot see well because of her
hood and gropes blindly.*

HYSTERECTOMY *is one of those people who spits copiously
and also has bad breath. She also shouts. Unfortunately,
she has a habit of sticking her face close to people and
bellows the following lines with her face right up to*
OEDOCLES, *who gets the full blast.*

HYSTERECTOMY What means this, noble King Oedocles? Why
do you weep by this sheet-shrouded figure on the bier?

OEDOCLES *(flinching and surreptitiously wiping his eye)* I
am glad you asked that question, fair Hysterectomy. Alas—

*He is interrupted by the late arrival of a member of
the* **CHORUS.**

—alas, I weep for my wife and your queen, the lovely Ovary.

The corpse sneezes.

HYSTERECTOMY Queen Ovary dead? How did this terrible
event occur? Was she murdered by political rivals or struck
down by the gods for some hideous sin?

OEDOCLES Neither, noble Hysterectomy. She ate some bad
fish. A piece of hake, to be precise.

HYSTERECTOMY Oh fatal hake, oh wretched fish so vile, foul
poisoner of our most beloved queen!

During the following, the **CHORUS** *become more and
more violent. Eventually, they fling themselves down
by* **OVARY**'s *body and start wailing and pummelling it
with their fists in distress.*

CHORUS Oh woe, thrice treble woe! Now let the seas

Boil over, and the sun conceal its face,

Let storms rage over every place on earth

May rivers flood until all life is drowned,

And hideous fires burn everything to ash.

If Ovary be dead, let all the earth

Be devastated to the very core.

OVARY *gives a cry of pain and half sits up.*

OEDOCLES Take up the body and bear my precious Queen Ovary to the burial place.

AMNESIA Come good King Oedocles, I will comfort thee in my sister's death.

HYSTERECTOMY Who is this grief-stricken female, who clutches your arm so fiercely?

OEDOCLES *(flinching)* The sister of my wife, Amnesia.

CHORUS Oh hapless sister! Was thou born for this?

Most miserable of women! Oh, most vile

And wretched in the earth! Oh woe to thee

Unhappiest of women! Surely thou

Art most accursed of all thy sex in Thebes.

The **CHORUS** *get violent again, weeping and tearing their clothes, and flinging themselves on* **AMNESIA**, *clutching her round the knees and beating at her. She emerges a wreck.*

OEDOCLES Thank you, fair women of Thebes, I'll let you know *(slight pause)* how much I am beholden for your sympathy. Take up the bier.

The two slaves do so. Unfortunately, the base of the stretcher gives way with a rending noise, and they are left holding two poles with the body still on the ground.

After a short pause, **OVARY**, *the body, realises what has happened and decides to save the situation. She therefore stands up in a crouching position, carefully* *keeping herself covered by the sheet, and moves off bent double inside the poles of the stretcher as it is carried off, the bearers indicating great grief and "oh, what a weight", etc.* OEDOCLES, AMNESIA *and* SCROTUM *follow sorrowfully. If the slaves are cut, the* CHORUS *can carry out the body, using the same business.*

HYSTERECTOMY *(to the* CHORUS, *showering them with saliva)*
Let us follow the bier and by the grave chant sad songs of sorrow.

CHORUS *(retaliating)* Ay, sad songs of sorrow shall it be.

HYSTERECTOMY *and the* CHORUS *exit after the bier and the others.*

Slow fade.

Scene Two

The same.

OEDOCLES *and* **AMNESIA** *enter, sobbing. They have just returned from the funeral.*

OEDOCLES My Ovary dead and buried these two hours!

Oh gods, now take away the memory

And help me to forget this dreadful thing.

The horror did not strike me until now.

He sobs bitterly and collapses in **AMNESIA**'s *arms. She comforts him.*

AMNESIA Good Oedocles, put some stop upon thy grief. While I yet live you always have a friend in me. I shall comfort you.

OEDOCLES *(misunderstanding)* You will?

AMNESIA I hold you dear upon my heart and shall try to be to you as my sister was in everything.

OEDOCLES Everything?

AMNESIA Of course. In everything.

OEDOCLES O Amnesia, this happiness is too much for one man. Joy fills my heart. For many years I longed to have this pleasure. Yet never did I think that it would come. And on such occasion as this.

AMNESIA What mean you?

OEDOCLES O let us wait no longer. What better place than here to consummate our love. *(He seizes her)*

AMNESIA You misunderstand me. Let me go. I love you as a sister.

OEDOCLES *(inflamed)* Never! I sense the hidden passion in your eyes. Your...your...your... *(He dries up)*

AMNESIA *points to her breasts.*

Ah, yes, your marble breasts inflame me. Your...your...your...

AMNESIA *points vaguely to her hips.*

(hopefully) ...bowels?

AMNESIA *points savagely again.* **OEDOCLES** *gets the message.*

Your hips! Yes, your lovely hips incite me to passion. *(He puts his hands on them)*

AMNESIA Let me go! The gods will be angry. Help! Help! *(She forces his hands away and flees)*

OEDOCLES I must have her though the heavens fall.

OEDOCLES *pursues* **AMNESIA** *offstage. She is heard screeching.*

CHORUS *enter.*

HYSTERECTOMY Oh woeful day! See where the envious king Pursues Amnesia through the astonished trees.

CHORUS 1 He has seized her by the waist.

CHORUS 2 She struggles to get free!

CHORUS 3 He has flung her on the ground.

CHORUS 1 Behold how he tears her clothes from her.

CHORUS 2 See! He lifts his tunic!

CHORUS 3 Ye gods, what is this terrible thing! Oh horrid sight!

They cover their faces in distress.

HYSTERECTOMY Behold, it is over!

CHORUS So soon?

HYSTERECTOMY The greatest crimes are swiftly carried out. See where King Oedocles, now satiate,

Has left the garden, while Amnesia,

Distraught and weeping wanders to and fro.

AMNESIA enters, crawling, banging her head on the ground, and exhibiting deep distress.

AMNESIA Woe! Woe! Unclean! Unclean! Oh, evil deed! What shall I do? I am of all women most accursed. Oh gods, reveal some escape from my shame. What are these women doing here with looks so wild? Who are you, pray?

HYSTERECTOMY *(thrusting her face close)* We are the women of Thebes, good Amnesia.

AMNESIA *(recoiling)* Then help me, citizens of Thebes. You know what happened, then?

HYSTERECTOMY We saw all of it. It was a horrid thing. You must have felt it deeply.

HYSTERECTOMY pursues the retreating AMNESIA.

AMNESIA Indeed I have never felt anything like it before. But how can I be cleansed in the sight of the gods?

HYSTERECTOMY Nearby this spot there is an old priestess

A devotee of Herbivore, Goddess

Of Gardens. We shall go to visit her,

And she will tell you what you have to do.

AMNESIA I thank thee, good woman of Thebes.

HYSTERECTOMY Then let us go.

CHORUS Then let us go.

ALL exit, except one of the CHORUS who has gone to sleep, standing up. HYSTERECTOMY returns and drags her off.

Scene Three

The same.

An old crone enters, cackling to show she is (a) a crone and (b) old. It is the PRIESTESS. *But* AMNESIA *is late appearing. After a preliminary reconnaissance, the* PRIESTESS *backs offstage, still cackling.*

AMNESIA *enters in a hurry.*

The PRIESTESS *peers out to make sure she's there and then resumes cackling and enters.*

PRIESTESS Where is the unhappy Amnesia?

AMNESIA Pray excellent elderly female, who may you be?

PRIESTESS I am the Priestess of Herbivore, Goddess of Gardens. They say you sought me. What do you want?

AMNESIA I am Amnesia, sister of the late Queen Ovary. After the funeral, her husband King Oedocles, maddened by lust, seized me and raped me in the garden. I still shudder at the memory of that awful thing. O, tell me what I must do to be cleansed.

The PRIESTESS *has a habit of wandering about the stage, cackling, and* AMNESIA *has to follow her.*

PRIESTESS I know all about it. The oracle told me.

AMNESIA What else said the oracle?

PRIESTESS Perhaps.

AMNESIA Perhaps what?

PRIESTESS Perhaps you will be cleansed if you devote the rest of your life to the goddess Herbivore. Take these. *(She hands her large garden shears)* They are the sacred secateurs of Herbivore. Use them to cut off from Oedocles those organs of generation where he shall have hopes of increase.

AMNESIA You mean—

PRIESTESS *(nodding)* No less.

AMNESIA Both?

PRIESTESS Ay. Take the offending globes and bring them back here to bury in the earth. From them will spring up a grove of trees, sacred to Herbivore, and you will spend your life tending it. Then the sin will be expiated and you will be cleansed.

AMNESIA I thank thee, kind priestess. I shall do as you direct and return.

PRIESTESS Do so. And bring back the secateurs.

AMNESIA I will. Farewell.

> **AMNESIA** *exits.*

> *Instant blackout, too quick for the* **PRIESTESS** *who can be heard blundering around looking for a way out and calling "I can't see" or something similar.*

> **OEDOCLES** *comes on in the blackout and trips over the* **PRIESTESS**.

> *We hear a loud shout and a noise as both fall. Immediately the lights go up to reveal* **OEDOCLES** *getting up and the* **PRIESTESS** *trying to crawl off on all fours.* **OEDOCLES** *gives a start of surprise but speedily adopts a heroic posture.*

Scene Four

The same.

OEDOCLES *discovered.*

OEDOCLES I am the happiest of men on earth!

He is interrupted by the **PRIESTESS**, *still crawling, cackling her way offstage.*

The beautiful Amnesia sends to say

That of her recent coyness she repents

And wishes to meet me here this afternoon.

The Rites of Aphrodite shall take place

And this time she shall willingly perform

Her part. Indeed I am most blessed of men.

AMNESIA *enters, holding shears concealed behind her back.*

AMNESIA *(passionately)* Oedocles!

OEDOCLES Amnesia!

AMNESIA You see I have come as I promised.

OEDOCLES *(seizing her)* I cannot wait to make you mine. But what are you holding in your hand? *(He indicates the shears)*

AMNESIA I promised an old friend to take a cutting from the garden and bring it back to her. *(She strokes him)* Shall we go seek it in the deepest part of the wood, where none shall see us? Oh, Oedocles, I cannot wait to be alone. I am so sorry you caught me unawares before. *(Fancying herself as a seductress, she rather overdoes it, stroking* **OEDOCLES**'s *bare thigh lasciviously)*

OEDOCLES *(beating her off; muttering)* My wife's here tonight. *(He retreats in embarrassment)* Perhaps I was too hasty. It will be different this time.

AMNESIA Ay, it will be different this time.

OEDOCLES Come, let us go. Aphrodite awaits.

They go out.

The **CHORUS** *enter.*

HYSTERECTOMY Now see the gods assemble for revenge!
And foolish Oedocles thinks in the woods
His love with her will consummated be.
Alas, a different fate awaits him now.

The **CHORUS** *face offstage and describe what they see.*

CHORUS See how they lie together on the ground.
She smiles her sweetest smiles at him and he
Lifts up his costly tunic as before.
But O, what horrid vision have we here?

HYSTERECTOMY While Oedocles is overwhelmed by love
Amnesia puts forth her little hand
And snatches up from by her side the Shears
Of Herbivore and with a cry she strikes.

OEDOCLES *(offstage)* WHURP!

CHORUS Oh horror, horror! See, she flees, whilst he
Totters around, in helpless agony.
Alas, poor Oedocles, thou art destroyed.

*AMNESIA enters, holding a plate on which are resting
two golf balls, covered by a handkerchief.*

AMNESIA 'Tis done! The deed is expiated and the gods
revenged! Now I shall take the globes back to the priestess
to show her.

As **AMNESIA** *goes to exit she tilts the plate and the two
golf balls roll out on to the stage. If they are handy,*

she can pick them up. If not, she exits with as much dignity as she can muster. If they should fall among the **CHORUS**, *they probably play football with them in an effort to save the situation.*

CHORUS Thus cleansed is Amnesia herself

And the gods happy that it has been done.

But what of Oedocles?

Acurséd by the gods he wanders forth

Rejected and despised throughout the land.

See what results from hurting Apollo!

O woe. O woe.

All exit. Half go one way and half the other. They realise simultaneously something has gone wrong and both parties change tack, which results in further confusion. Eventually they dribble out.

Blackout.

Scene Five

A grove.

On one of the rostra there is now a small monument topped by two stone globes. It is a tombstone to what OEDOCLES *lost.*

OEDOCLES *and* SCROTUM *enter.* OEDOCLES *walks with a strange gait, suggesting somebody has done him an injury. He has aged considerably; indeed, it might be said he has rather overdone it. He wears a ghastly grey wig.*

OEDOCLES Here let us rest a while, good Scrotum. *(He sinks down on a rostrum near the tomb)* I wonder what this noble monument commemorates? That it should come to this, old friend. Once I was a king. Now they have cast me out because I am no longer capable of having an heir to the throne. Thus I am doomed to roam the earth eternally, knowing no peace.

CHORUS A *enters.*

CHORUS A Oedocles! I bring sad news, tidings of such despair I can scarce bear to utter them. May my tongue be cursed for saying so, but when your sweet sister heard you were no longer king, she hanged herself.

CHORUS A *exits.*

OEDOCLES Oh woe, woe that the gods should seek such cruel revenge.

CHORUS A *enters because she forgot to finish the line.*

CHORUS A And died.

CHORUS A *exits.*

OEDOCLES *(rising)* Have I not suffered enough? Oh, hateful day.

CHORUS B *enters.*

CHORUS B Oedocles! I bring even sadder news. When your mother heard your sister had hanged herself, she drank poison and expired hideously.

CHORUS B *exits.*

OEDOCLES Oh nine times nine times woe! Oh gods, be merciful!

CHORUS C *enters.*

CHORUS C Oedocles! Terrible tidings. When your father heard your mother had taken poison because your sister hanged herself, he threw himself from the highest tower in Thebes.

OEDOCLES And died?

CHORUS C He is nothing but a stain in the street.

CHORUS C *exits.*

OEDOCLES *(tottering)* Aaaah! Support me, good Scrotum. Why do the gods not kill me now?

SCROTUM Good cheer, my lord, that news was surely the last.

CHORUS D *enters.*

CHORUS D Oedocles! More news!

OEDOCLES What is it?

CHORUS D Both your grandparents. When they heard your father threw himself off the highest tower in Thebes because your mother took poison on learning your sister had hanged herself, they tied themselves together and jumped into the river.

OEDOCLES And drowned?

CHORUS D No.

OEDOCLES The gods be praised. They live?

CHORUS D They hit a rock and broke their necks.

CHORUS D *exits.*

OEDOCLES So all my loved ones dead? Oh thirty-three times woe, oh curse the day that I was born. *(He sobs)*

SCROTUM Be of good cheer, sir. The darkest cloud conceals the sun. I will sacrifice to Apollo. He may hear.

OEDOCLES Thanks, generous Scrotum. There is nothing in the world I value so much as my Scrotum. You have an honest heart, even though you are old and stinking.

SCROTUM *(fiercely)* Sinking.

OEDOCLES Sinking.

SCROTUM I am not stinking. I've never been so insulted in thirty years with the society. I shall withdraw my deed of covenant. Furthermore, if you—

CHORUS *enter, cutting him off. They are carrying leafy branches (well, it's a grove, isn't it?). One or two have misunderstood their instructions and have provided themselves with young tree trunks. They wave their branches to indicate the presence of trees.*

HYSTERECTOMY Oedocles! What are you doing here?

OEDOCLES I am doomed to wander by the gods as a punishment for my crime against Amnesia.

HYSTERECTOMY Amnesia is not far from here. She tends this grove of olive trees dedicated to Herbivore. Why not seek her out and ask forgiveness? Perchance the gods would relent.

OEDOCLES She would not see me.

HYSTERECTOMY I believe she would. Let me seek her. Amnesia! Amnesia!

HYSTERECTOMY *exits.*

CHORUS O dreadful fate for Oedocles the King.

He who bestrode the earth with mighty tread

Is now reduced to creeping like a snail.

O piteous sight! O fearful thing to watch!

The gods have punished him with mighty blows.

The **CHORUS** *exit.*

A sandal is left behind on stage. A hand comes out and tries to retrieve it unsuccessfully.

OEDOCLES *(tottering)* Ah! *(He clutches* **SCROTUM***)* Let me hold on to my Scrotum. I feel a sense of foreboding. All is darkness. I fear my time will not be long.

SCROTUM Have courage. She will come.

AMNESIA *enters.*

OEDOCLES *(rising)* Amnesia!

AMNESIA Who calls? Who are you, stranger? Know you not this grove is sacred to Herbivore? And why stand you so strangely?

OEDOCLES Oh Amnesia, you should know why I stand so strangely.

AMNESIA Can it be? Oedocles! And faithful Scrotum too.

OEDOCLES I have come to—

He is interrupted by a **CHORUS** *member coming in for her sandal. She picks it up, tiptoes off with great slowness and exaggerated caution and exits after what seems an eternity.*

I have come to seek forgiveness before I die. They tell me that some parts of me lie here.

AMNESIA Indeed they do. Behold their tiny graves. I myself had the memorial erected. *(She indicates the monument)*

OEDOCLES Is this the grave? My little globes! *(He kneels by the pitiful grave)*

AMNESIA Aye, Oedocles, your globes. And from their grave has sprung this lovely olive grove, dedicated to the goddess Herbivore.

OEDOCLES May she forgive me!

AMNESIA Your pilgrimage has earned her forgiveness. And you have mine too.

OEDOCLES Then are the gods content and I most blessed of men! *(He sinks down by the grave, wincing a little)* Farewell, good Amnesia. Farewell, honest Scrotum. I die. Oh farewell, earth. Great Charon, I greet thee! Oh globes, I come! *(He dies at some length, but keeps reviving, gasping and falling back)*

AMNESIA *(when it is safe to approach the body)* Farewell, brave Oedocles.

OEDOCLES *(suddenly sitting up)* Farewell! *(He sinks back)*

> **AMNESIA** *gasps in surprise as this wasn't in the script, but controls herself.*

> **HYSTERECTOMY** *and* **CHORUS** *enter.*

> **HYSTERECTOMY** *kneels by* **OEDOCLES**. *During the following, she places her face close to his and showers spit and bad breath over the body, which is eventually forced to turn out of the way.*

HYSTERECTOMY Oh, what a sight is this upon the ground!

Brave Oedocles is dead and by his globes.

CHORUS Oh woe that gallant Oedocles is dead.

O dreadful sight. O woe, O triple woe.

AMNESIA See he is buried by his globes. Let them be reunited in death. The curse is lifted. Let us all go in.

CHORUS Farewell, O Oedocles of Thebes the King.

This happens when the gods they are defied.

O four times, five times woe and yet more woe.

The **CHORUS** *work themselves up to a final paroxysm and hurl their leafy branches on* **OEDOCLES**, *and then hurl themselves with cries of "Woe". He groans in pain.*

Slow fade.

The End

PRIDE AT SOUTHANGER PARK

PRIDE AT SOUTHANGER PARK

Adapted for the stage from
Jane Austen's long-lost work

by Rupert Bean

First performed by the Old Carthusian Dramatic Society at
The Redgrave Theatre, Farnham, on 8th March, 1998, as part
of the Tenth Coarse Acting Festival, with the following cast:

CECILY CHICHESTER, an orphan	Claire Mistry
LADY FANNY BOTTOMLEY, Cecily's aunt	Suzy Winter
REVEREND GILES HENRY, a vicar	Ashley Pannell
GLADYS, the maid	Clare Croome
SIR THOMAS BOTTOMLEY, Cecily's uncle	Murray Pannell
WILLIAM SQUIRES, a suitor	Rupert Bean
MRS SQUIRES, William's mother	Tom Chisman
MARCUS D'ANGELO, another suitor	Jake McQuitty
FRONT OF HOUSE MANAGER	Damien De Roche
DRUNKEN HUSBAND	Mike Aldridge

Directed by **Rupert Bean**
Lighting and Sound by **Nick Townsend**

Note: The drunken husband does not appear in the published
version. Mrs Squires and the front of house manager may both
be played by females.

PRODUCTION NOTES

For nearly twenty years The Redgrave Theatre, Farnham, put on a Coarse Acting Competition every other year to raise money, and this play was an entry in the last competition in 1998. Soon afterwards, the theatre sadly went dark, though one hopes not for ever. As usual, I was adjudicating the competition and I was much impressed by this piece. However, I somehow got the idea that the author, Rupert Bean, and his team from the Old Carthusian Dramatic Society, had won the competition two years previously, so I did not award it first prize. That turned out to be a typical piece of Coarse adjudication, because they hadn't won two years previously; somebody else had come first and author Rupert Bean had then got the award for best director.

I was therefore very happy to make amends by including it in this book, especially because it was greeted with uproarious laughter at The Redgrave. Since then, one or two alterations have been made. In the original, Mrs Squires was played by a man (the Carthusians are one of the few drama groups to have a surplus of men). As this volume aims to give more opportunities for women, that restriction has been removed. However, this doesn't mean Mrs Squires needn't be played by a man–if you have one to spare (see notes on the characters).

As regards the rest of the production, Rupert Bean recommends there should be a great sense of BBC Jane Austen about the whole thing. Costumes and set should be as circa 1820 as possible (except the outrageous Reverend). However, they haven't quite got things right, as witness the music. This is a production by someone who's seen the TV series but hasn't read the book (or any books probably). The cast make a great effort at the period style, bowing, fluttering fans, etc., but they haven't much of a clue.

The interruptions by the house manager will be much funnier if the cast react by stopping, freezing and staring bleakly at her. If they play through regardless, the business won't be funny because the audience's attention will be split. We want to feel that there will be a row afterwards ("I don't care about the audience, you spoilt my big moment..."). The house manager herself, like all front of house staff, is unaware of the effect of the interruption. Incidentally, she must be at the front of the audience or she won't be seen. And you must have a stooge planted for the person whose ticket she challenges, otherwise a real argument may develop. The whole business must go quickly and smoothly or the atmosphere will be wrecked. The same applies to her second entrance with ice creams.

As for the easy chair, the breaking of which causes so much trouble towards the end of the piece, use an old chair from a rubbish tip or charity shop so the leg can be sawn off. The length cut off will depend on the thickness of the Bible which replaces it. Balance the chair with the cut-off piece and cover the whole thing with ornate wraps and so on. Then it will collapse when Cecily walks into it; this is essential, as much of the plot depends on it. If it doesn't work for Cecily, somebody else must find an excuse for making it collapse. Rehearse it frequently. Don't leave it to the dress rehearsal.

Michael Green

NOTES ON THE CHARACTERS

CECILY CHICHESTER, an 18-year-old orphan: Very attractive actress. Keen, new acquisition to the group. Anxious to shine.

SIR THOMAS BOTTOMLEY, Cecily's uncle: Played by a young actor who thinks his character should be grandiose and pompous. His real-life wife is about to give birth, so he is armed with a (concealed) mobile phone. Very highly strung and can't take crises, especially now.

LADY FANNY BOTTOMLEY, Thomas's wife. Actually quite a decent actress, though let down by the incompetents around her.

REVEREND GILES HENRY, the vicar: Thinks that as a churchman he should carry a Bible and crucifix; tends to cross the air for no reason whatsoever; he is also wearing some sort of papal outfit, preferably bright red, since this was the only costume remotely religious that the wardrobe had.

WILLIAM SQUIRES, Cecily's tutor: Can't act for toffee and only given the role because his dad gave £500 to the Society. Suffers bad stage fright.

MRS SQUIRES, William's mother: If played by a woman, she should have a "common" accent but try to talk posh. A bad piece of casting, but there was no one else. However, the part can be played by a man, in which case he should do his Widow Twanky performance from last year's *Aladdin*.

MARCUS D'ANGELO, loveable rogue and suitor: Modelled on the sexy Mr Darcy of Colin Firth in the 1998 TV production of *Pride and Prejudice*, complete with sideburns and tight trousers. Very full of himself. Tends to address all his lines to the audience.

GLADYS, the maid: Coarse actress from the Midlands, complete with chip on her shoulder. Keen to develop the role.

FRONT OF HOUSE MANAGER: This part should be played by an actress, not the real person. Armed with a powerful voice and torch to match. Has no idea of the destruction she is causing with her ill-judged interventions.

The action at the play takes place in the living room of Southanger Park, the ancestral seat of Sir Thomas and Lady Fanny Bottomley in Hampshire.

Scene One

*Lights down. The soundtrack from **"GONE WITH THE WIND (TARA'S THEME)"** is played–a fuzzy recording. According to the director, this gives the piece the "epic quality" it needs to be up there with National Theatre productions. How wrong can one man be.*

Lights up on the living-room of Southanger Park. Chaise-longue, an armchair (see production notes), and a table with flowers set; plus anything else one feels would look at home in a Jane Austen epic. The entrance to the room is right; the exit to the dining room is left.

CECILY CHICHESTER, *just turned 18, is standing looking out at the audience as if though a window. She has forgotten to take her watch off. She is constantly using her fan.*

LADY FANNY BOTTOMLEY *is sitting on the chaise longue, stroking an obviously fake toy dog.*

The music continues, since the sound engineer is having an argument with the lighting man about football.

There is an awkward pause while the two actresses exchange worried glances.

CECILY *decides to start anyway, shouting loudly to be heard over the music.*

CECILY Dear aunt, now that I have turned eighteen, can I be allowed to marry whom I choose?

LADY FANNY Cecily my child, you know how strict your uncle, Sir Thomas, is–he will need to approve of the match.

CECILY But what about love? Does that not count for anything?

LADY FANNY What of that virtue?

CECILY turns and runs to LADY FANNY, as the music cuts out with a screech. They look plainly relieved.

CECILY Surely I must be allowed to marry someone whom I truly love?

LADY FANNY But you will learn to love in time. Love must be initially forsaken in favour of family, status and security.

CECILY So this is why my uncle has invited the odious Mrs Squires and her son to my birthday dinner here tonight. He wishes me to consider Mr Squires as a suitable posster...

There is a pause.

...possible suitor.

By now the FRONT OF HOUSE MANAGER has strolled in, armed with her loud voice and powerful torch. (One of the laws of Coarse Acting is that the FOH staff are always more audible than the cast).

She bounds up to a person on the aisle, sweeps the torch around and settles on their face. (See production notes.) During this interruption, LADY FANNY and CECILY glare pointedly at the FOH MANAGER, angry at the hiatus.

FOH MANAGER *(booming)* Excuse me, sir, can I see your ticket please?

There is some protesting.

Well, I'm sorry, sir, but this ticket is for next week's matinée performance of Mother Courage. Because of you, we have had to turn people away. Please see me in the interval.

FOH MANAGER *retreats, though not before sweeping the audience once more with the torch.*

The play continues. **LADY FANNY** *gets up very quickly, forgetting the dog on her lap which just falls on the floor. She replaces the dog on the sofa.*

LADY FANNY I do not believe that there is any consideration to do, child. Ever since your parents died, Sir Thomas has felt it his duty to marry you off to someone of high social standing.

WILLIAM Squires is such a man, and you could do far worse.

CECILY But aunt...

Pause. The doorbell rings, as electric sounding as possible, preferably with a silly tune.

LADY FANNY Hush, child, for Gladys will shortly enter with the first of our guests.

Huge pause. **GLADYS** *does no such thing.*

(ad-libbing) Surely I hear Gladys in the hall with the first of our guests?

The doorbell sounds again. **REVEREND GILES HENRY** *can be heard offstage.*

REVEREND *(offstage)* If she's not here, I'll just go on, shall I?

The **REVEREND** *struts on stage right. He is equipped with a Bible, a crucifix around his neck, and is wearing full bishop regalia, complete with mitre. As soon as he enters, he crosses the air, as he feels all holy men do this every waking moment. Indeed, he has spent the last three Sundays before performance in church studying the vicar.*

(to non-existent **GLADYS***)* Thank you, my good woman; may your soul have eternal salvation.

It should be noted that the **REVEREND** *has not bothered to learn his lines. He has craftily inserted bits of his script into his enormous Bible. ("No one will notice a thing old chap").*

Suddenly **GLADYS** *appears right and makes a late, lame attempt to show the* **REVEREND** *into the room. She wears a cap that is too small for her.*

Thank you, my good woman; may your soul have eternal salvation. *(He then tries to shoo her offstage)*

As **GLADYS** *moves to exit, her minute cap falls off. She picks it up.*

GLADYS *(moving to the exit right)* I was helping *(name of actor playing* **SIR THOMAS***)* with his costume—can't be in two bleedin' places at the same time, can I?

GLADYS *exits right.*

Awkward pause. The cast valiantly continue in earnest.

LADY FANNY *(going to* **REVEREND***)* Reverend Henry, how good of you to make Cecily's celebrations this evening.

REVEREND *(opening the Bible for the lines)* My pleasure, Lady Bottomley. May I take this opportunity to bid Miss Chichester welcome to the world of adulthood both literal and spiritual. I hope I will have the continued pleasure of having her.

Another awkward pause. **CECILY** *indicates to the* **REVEREND** *to turn over the page.*

(realising) of having her attend my services at St Bartholomew's.

CECILY But, Reverend, how can you condone—

LADY FANNY Hush, child, your uncle is coming. Let us hear no more of this.

They all swivel expectantly, as if on strings, to right, but **SIR THOMAS** *enters left. Unknown to the rest of the cast, he has on his person a mobile phone, in case his real life wife goes into labour. He is obviously a young man overly made up to look old, with padding and huge grey sideburns.*

SIR THOMAS Ah, Reverend, so glad you could join us.

The three others all immediately swing round to look at him. The two swivels should be very fast and slick.

REVEREND A pleasure as always, Sir Thomas.

SIR THOMAS *(to* **CECILY***)* My dear child, shortly Mrs Squires from William Hill will join us with her son Burrow...

Pause as he realises the mix-up.

(continuing) Mrs Squires from Burrow Hill will join us with her son William. I have high hopes that he will prove a perfect match for you.

CECILY *looks shocked, fanning herself and holding her hand to her brow.*

LADY FANNY My husband, when are they expected?

SIR THOMAS I told them eight of the clock.

Instinctively, everyone looks at their wrists. **CECILY** *realises that her watch is still on, so she quickly removes it and throws it offstage. It hits* **GLADYS**.

GLADYS *(offstage)* Ow–what are you playing at?

The watch is hurled back at **CECILY** *with vehement force.*

LADY FANNY No doubt they are purposefully arriving tardily to make an impression on the young Cecily. *(She sits down on the chaise-longue, squashing the dog. She subtly extracts the dog and places it on her lap)*

REVEREND Ah, the tricks that those in love do play upon the objects of their affection. *(He crosses the air for no apparent reason)*

CECILY But uncle, I do not love William Squires, for all his supposed wealth.

SIR THOMAS *(angrily)* What? You dare defy my wishes, child? You dare to disobey your uncle?

REVEREND Cecily, Cecily, stop crying.

She hasn't even started...she does now.

You are revolting.

There is a pause. **CECILY** *stops crying momentarily and indicates for the page to be turned. She then continues to weep.*

You are revolting...against your uncle, which cannot be advised. Please allow this dinner to proceed, and maybe your heart's desires will shine in Mr Squires' direction.

CECILY *(crying and sitting down)* Never!

SIR THOMAS Sit down!

CECILY *stands up and sits down again. The electric doorbell rings.*

LADY FANNY Ah, our final two guests have graced us with their presence.

GLADYS *enters, wearing her tiny cap again.*

GLADYS Mrs Squires and her son Mr William Squires.

MRS SQUIRES *enters right with* **WILLIAM,** *who can't act to save his life and is plainly terrified, indicated by his visible shaking and the fact that he finishes a cigarette which he hands to a disembodied hand offstage.*

SIR THOMAS Thank you, Gladys, that will be all. Please inform cook that dinner can be served.

GLADYS *does not move or speak, as directed* **SIR THOMAS** *decides to soldier on anyway.*

Mrs Squires, how delightful to...

GLADYS *now comes to life.*

GLADYS *(interrupting)* Yes, sir. *(As she moves to the exit right, her cap falls off. She picks it up)* My part's too small, my cap's too small, it's pathetic.

GLADYS *exits.*

SIR THOMAS *looks daggers after her.*

SIR THOMAS Mrs Squires, how delightful to see you again.

MRS SQUIRES Oh Sir Thomas, the pleasure is all ours, isn't it, William?

WILLIAM, *who has been staring transfixed out at the audience, looks blankly (no doubt suffering from Green's Syndrome).*

WILLIAM Er...yes, that's right.

SIR THOMAS William, may I present Miss Cecily Chichester, my niece.

WILLIAM *steps towards* **CECILY,** *consciously mouthing "one, two, three", as the director has told him to move three steps.*

WILLIAM *(woodenly)* How do you do, Miss... Miss... Miss Winchester.

ALL *(sotto voce)* Chichester.

WILLIAM Chichester.

MRS SQUIRES I 'ope we can make a marriage union at the table 'ere this evening.

SIR THOMAS As do we all, Mrs Squires. Then Reverend Henry can perhaps perform the ceremony in this very room tonight!

Everyone, except **CECILY,** *laughs heartily (though incredibly falsely) at this feeble joke. Someone breaks wind incredibly audibly (use a whoopee cushion offstage). In actual fact* **SIR THOMAS** *is the culprit, and so everyone starts edging away from him and the women fan themselves even more vigorously.*

GLADYS *enters right, wearing the small cap again, which falls off immediately. She leaves it there, but kicks it in frustration.*

GLADYS Dinner is served.

GLADYS *moves from right to left and off left all the time with her left hand extended, as if indicating where everyone should go off.*

SIR THOMAS, LADY FANNY *and* **MRS SQUIRES** *exit, muttering "Rhubarb, rhubarb" etc.* **LADY FANNY** *takes the dog with her, but then decides she should leave it behind. She throws it back on to the chaise-longue before exiting.*

WILLIAM *walks over to* **CECILY,** *while the* **REVEREND** *stands at the back.*

WILLIAM Oh Cecily, I feel such affinity for you that I cannot express its true worth.

How true, since a carrot could produce a more convincing performance.

CECILY Oh Mr Squires, I do not love you, and never will. Please refrain from making further overtures of such fervent emotion to me.

WILLIAM I cannot promise. However, your uncle wishes us wed whatever the cost, so you had better become accustomed to the idea, Miss... Miss... Colchester.

CECILY
REVEREND } *(together)* Chichester.

WILLIAM Chichester. *(He moves to the wrong exit, right)*

CECILY *and the* **REVEREND** *point him to the exit left.*

WILLIAM *exits left.*

CECILY Oh Reverend, am I alone in believing, of ever hoping, in the cardinal virtue of true everlasting love and in confirming true love vows in the sanctity of the holy church?

REVEREND My dear Cecily, you can hold to that ecclesiastical belief, you dog.

Pause. **CECILY** *indicates for him to turn over the page. He does so.*

You can hold to that ecclesiastical belief, you dog-matic child, but heaven help you for going against your uncle's wishes. But haste, we must follow into supper.

The **REVEREND** *slams his Bible shut with determination and strides off left unknown to* **CECILY**, *who is staring romantically out at the audience.*

CECILY Reverend, before we do...

The **REVEREND** *dashes back in.*

...let me relate to you my plan. I have of late met a wonderful and caring man of good character and respectable income. His name is Marcus D'Angelo. *(She turns quickly and bangs her shin against the leg of the chair that has been set to break and now comes off. Clearly in agony, she continues her lines, but has difficulty remaining upright)* I have arranged for him to arrive after supper and then I hope my uncle can see for himself what an excellent match he is for me.

REVEREND *(crossing the air for no reason)* I will support you in any way I can.

The **REVEREND** *has to literally support* **CECILY** *on the way out.*

The music starts again.

Blackout.

Scene Two

The same, a few hours later.

Lights up. The music fades on time (for once), albeit with a hiss and a squeak.

MARCUS D'ANGELO, *played by a keen actor who has seen Colin Firth's Mr Darcy far too many times for his own good, struts on stage from right, groin thrust out. Heavy sideburns attached (to his face, not the groin).*

MARCUS Thank you for showing me in, Gladys; if you could kindly... *(He looks around for* **GLADYS***)*

No sign of her.

MARCUS *exits.*

(offstage) For heaven's sake, where is she? *(Beat)* Well, get her out of there. I've got people from the BBC here tonight.

MARCUS *comes on again.*

GLADYS *is hurled on stage right, wearing a huge cap which covers her eyes. She cannot see where she is going and has to grab on to* **MARCUS***'s groin to maintain some stability.*

MARCUS *fends her off.*

(to the audience) Thank you for showing me in, Gladys; if you could kindly inform Sir Thomas and his party...

GLADYS Yes, sir. *(She makes to leave)*

MARCUS *grabs her.*

MARCUS ...that Mr Marcus D'Angelo has arrived and presents his compliments.

GLADYS Yes, sir. *(She moves to exit left. She mutters under her breath)* Pompous sod.

GLADYS *exits.*

MARCUS *struts around, suddenly conscious that one of his sideburns is coming off. He tries to sit on the chair, but then realises it is broken. He moves around again, and then sits down on the sofa, squashing the toy dog. He rises once more.*

CECILY *enters left.*

CECILY Mr D'Angelo!

She runs to him, and they kiss fakely, but passionately, making Coarse noises.

As soon as everyone is assembled, we will see what my uncle has to say, my darling.

MARCUS My only wish is to become your husband, dear Cecily.

REVEREND HENRY *enters, crosses the air, and shakes* **MARCUS***'s hand.*

REVEREND *(opening the Bible)* Mr D'Angelo, I presume? My name is Reverend Henry... Giles... Henry... Giles Henry, friend to Sir Thomas and Lady Fanny Bottomley. May you be blessed with eternal salvation and everlasting light.

The stage is suddenly plunged into darkness. **MARCUS** *can be heard speaking to someone offstage.*

MARCUS *(offstage)* What's happening? *(Beat)* No, I don't have a spare filament. Tell him to get those lights up again.

The lights come up again.

MARCUS *enters.*

Reverend, has Miss Chichester revealed her intentions to you?

The side doors now open, and the **FOH MANAGER** *enters with a refreshments trolley, and the torch of course.*

FOH MANAGER *(booming)* Ice creams... Oh, sorry, I thought it was the interval when the lights came down. Sorry, my fault.

FOH MANAGER *backs off whence she came.*

The players valiantly continue.

REVEREND That she has, and she has indicated that your assets are in no way small.

MARCUS *is now holding his sideburn constantly.*

MARCUS That is correct, Reverend. I have a modest income which I trust will keep Miss Chichester in the manner to which she is accustomed.

SIR THOMAS *and* **LADY FANNY** *enter left, the latter rescuing her toy dog from the chaise-longue.*

SIR THOMAS *(angrily)* What is the meaning of this intrusion? Who sir, are you, sir?

During the following speech, **SIR THOMAS** *attempts to sit down on the broken seat. Realising one leg is broken, he looks for an object to go under the leg. He grabs the Bible from* **REVEREND HENRY**, *who is now stuck, since all his lines are in the good book Panic is clearly etched on* **REVEREND**'s *face, and he will henceforth make lame attempts to get the book back, to no avail.*

MARCUS My name is Marcus D'Angelo, Sir Thomas. I have recently moved into the area from Canterbury where my father was a wealthy landowner. After his death, I moved here with my mother and my two sisters. I have become a partner in a local legal practice and have bought a small house with my wage.

SIR THOMAS All that is well and good, Mr D'Angelo, but Cecily already has a respectable suitor.

MARCUS Is he here at this time?

LADY FANNY Not yet, but let us ring for Gladys to bring William and his mother in.

MARCUS *(under his breath)* You'll be lucky.

> **LADY FANNY** *looks around for the bell on the side table, but finds it has not been set.*

LADY FANNY Let us call her instead. Oh, Gladys! Gladys!

> *Pause.*

> *Eventually* **GLADYS** *enters right, still wearing the cap which covers her entire head.*

GLADYS I was waiting for the bell cue, wasn't I?

LADY FANNY Gladys, please ask Mrs Squires and William to join us–I believe they are in the garden.

GLADYS Yes, sir...madam.

> **GLADYS** *exits left, tripping as she can't see where she's going.*

SIR THOMAS Reverend Henry, while we wait for the other guests, what is your opinion on this matter? The viewpoint of a man of the cloth is of crucial import to me.

> *Everyone turns expectantly to* **REVEREND HENRY**. *He looks blank.*

> *Pause.*

REVEREND *(ad-libbing)* I was afraid you would ask me that, Sir Thomas. I feel we must leave it to the Lord God Almighty to decide. *(He crosses the air)*

SIR THOMAS *is surprised, since the* REVEREND *was supposed to have a speech lasting two pages.*

SIR THOMAS Er, right, well, I understand all your many arguments, both on the spiritual and lay sides and I appreciate your candour in recommending the path of true love, and therefore Mr D'Angelo. However, I feel that we must hear Mr Squires speak first.

GLADYS *enters left, tripping everywhere.*

GLADYS The Squires.

MRS SQUIRES *and* WILLIAM *enter left.*

GLADYS *stays on stage this time, but stumbles around, unable to see.*

MRS SQUIRES Sir Thomas, with your permission, let us confirm this wedding match.

MARCUS *looks shocked, and turns to the audience for an aside.*

MARCUS That man is familiar to me–I must try and remember the circumstances.

WILLIAM *goes to* CECILY *and takes her hands in his own, visibly shaking with fright.*

WILLIAM *(woodenly)* Oh Cecily, will you accept my proposal of marriage, since my heart is full to overflowing with passion for you.

CECILY I can almost feel that passion permeating my soul, but I am afraid that it cannot be returned. My heart belongs to another and Reverend Henry always told me to follow my heart's teachings.

WILLIAM *turns to where the* REVEREND *should be, but finds an empty space, since the* REVEREND *has been edging over to the chair to retrieve his lines.*

WILLIAM Is this true, Reverend?

REVEREND *(with no clue)* I don't know...er...yes, that's true, I did.

CECILY Oh, but you did, you did!

> *Huge pause. The* **REVEREND** *indicates that his lines are in the Bible holding up the sofa.*

> *At this point,* **MARCUS** *is supposed to step in with his momentous line, but he has forgotten his cue in his desire to stand heroically looking out at the audience. In addition,* **GLADYS** *has now bumped into him and he is trying to get rid of her.* **WILLIAM** *decides to step in, clearly in terror.*

WILLIAM My heart is full to overflowing with passion for you.

CECILY I can almost feel that passion permeating my soul, but I am afraid that it cannot be returned. My heart belongs to another and Reverend Henry always told me to follow my heart's teachings.

WILLIAM *(in panic)* Is this true, Reverend?

REVEREND *(now completely lost)* Yes, that's true, I did.

CECILY Oh, but you did, you did!

> **MARCUS** *still fails to step in.* **WILLIAM** *moves in again, and the circle begins once more.*

WILLIAM My heart is full to overflowing with passion for you.

CECILY *(still with feeling, if not more so)* I can almost feel that passion permeating my soul, but I am afraid that it cannot be returned. My heart belongs to another and Reverend Henry always told me to follow my heart's teachings.

WILLIAM *(about to cry)* Is this true, Reverend?

REVEREND *(giving up)* No, no, I did not.

CECILY Oh, but you did, you did!

MARCUS *is finally jolted into action by whoever is nearest him.*

MARCUS *(to* WILLIAM*)* You!

LADY FANNY *(clearly relieved that the play is back on track)* Oh, thank God...er, I mean, you know him?

MARCUS If I am not mistaken, this is the man whom I have seen squandering his money in illegal card games and on women of the town.

LADY FANNY *faints Coarsely (making sure she is not hurt), dropping the dog on the floor. Everyone turns to the* REVEREND, *who is supposed to have lines here. He shrugs and crosses the air.*

MRS SQUIRES Oh William, your passionate emotions will be the death of you.

WILLIAM *(with zero vigour)* But I deny these charges vigorously, Mother.

SIR THOMAS Could you swear upon Reverend Henry's Bible, William?

In the original production, "Bible" was pronounced "By-Bell". For some reason, everyone laughed.

WILLIAM Certainly. *(He moves to the* REVEREND*)*

The REVEREND *points out the location of his Bible.* WILLIAM *gets down on his hands and knees and puts his hand on the Bible. He pauses and tries to act pained, but comes across as having a bad case of wind.*

I cannot. The act of blasphemy would tear my very soul apart. I admit Mr D'Angelo's charges.

MRS SQUIRES *(cuffing* WILLIAM*)* Oh, how could you, William?

WILLIAM Sorry, Mother, but with so much pent-up emotion I could not help myself.

CECILY *(to* SIR THOMAS*)* Oh uncle, I await your decision as to whom I can marry, but I hope and pray you can see where my love lies.

SIR THOMAS *rises, allowing the* REVEREND *to retrieve the Bible and thus his lines.*

SIR THOMAS My dear niece Cecily, for the last eight years you have lived under our roof...

Suddenly his mobile phone rings. He tries to ignore it at first, but eventually has to answer it. There is a pause as he answers. GLADYS *is in hysterics.*

She's having contractions? Oh, my God, I'm on my way. *(He makes to rush out)*

CECILY *blocks his path.*

CECILY I *must* know your answer, Uncle.

SIR THOMAS Get out the way, Helen's gone into labour. *(He makes to go out the other way)*

MARCUS *blocks his path.*

MARCUS *Please,* Sir Thomas, may I have permission to wed Cecily?

SIR THOMAS I don't care, get out of the bloody way, she needs me.

MARCUS Just say yes.

SIR THOMAS YES! Now move.

SIR THOMAS *shoves* MARCUS *aside and rushes out.*

CECILY We can be together forever.

MARCUS My Cecily!

CECILY My Marcus!

They embrace, to such an extent that CECILY *has to fight him off, with comments such as "Cut it out, you cheeky sod". The* REVEREND *has now found his place in the Bible.*

REVEREND I shall be honoured to give you both my blessing, since it is obvious that you are both mad.

GLADYS *points out that he needs to turn over. He does so.*

...it is obvious that you are both mad...for each other.

SIR THOMAS *runs on, putting on his coat and speaking on his mobile again.*

SIR THOMAS *(into the phone)* Hell, I'm blocked in...look, tell her to take deep breaths like we did at pre-natal. Hang on... *(Directly to the audience)* Does anyone here own a blue Volvo estate, in poor condition, broken wing mirror...? No, oh, hell. *(He starts pacing the stage. Into the phone)* Put her on, put her on...well, get her off the floor then...

MARCUS Reverend, kindly bless this holy matrimony.

REVEREND HENRY *is trying really hard to hold things together as things become more and more chaotic. Meanwhile,* GLADYS *is stumbling around, tripping all over the shop.*

REVEREND Dearly beloved, by the power...

SIR THOMAS, *clearly desperate, suddenly rushes up to the* REVEREND, *calling the actor by his real name—adapt as required.*

SIR THOMAS Ashley, it's not your car, is it?

REVEREND *(ignoring him)* Dearly beloved, by the power...

SIR THOMAS *(desperately)* Ashley?

This is all too much for REVEREND HENRY *to take. Earnest Coarse Actor that he is, he responds to*

SIR THOMAS *as if he is singing a mediaeval monastic chant.*

REVEREND *(chanting and crossing the air)* Look, as you bloody well know I drive a red Ford Mondeo–I wouldn't be seen dead in a Volvo. Amen.

WILLIAM *and* **MRS SQUIRES** *have been standing in their places, unsure of what to do. They take action now.*

WILLIAM Let us leave, Mother, for I am so full of sorrow, I fear my heart will bleed.

MRS SQUIRES *(ad-libbing)* Good idea.

MRS SQUIRES *and* **WILLIAM** *exit right hurriedly.*

CECILY Reverend, what is happening? Marry us, *please.*

MARCUS *(out of character)* Actually, I think it's me.

CECILY *(completely confused and ad-libbing)* Yes, yes, *you* will be my husband.

MARCUS No, I think it's my car.

REVEREND Dearly beloved, by the power invested in me...

SIR THOMAS *now addresses the actor playing* **MARCUS** *by his real name–adapt as required.*

SIR THOMAS Oh, it's you, Jake, is it? Well, move it—it looks like triplets.

SIR THOMAS *dashes out.*

MARCUS Certainly, Sir Thomas, I will move my carriage that is hindering your retreat.

MARCUS *runs out right, leaving* **CECILY** *alone.*

REVEREND *(loudly, above the din)* Dearly beloved, by the power invested in me... Oh sod this for a laugh...

The **REVEREND** *exits in a huff.* **GLADYS** *is still onstage in hysterics.*

LADY FANNY *crawls off.*

CECILY *tiptoes out* right.

GLADYS *moves forward to take her bow. Lights down and music.*

During the curtain call, the **FOH MANAGER** *gives flowers to* **GLADYS** *who has cleverly positioned herself in the centre of the row.* **CECILY** *angrily grabs them from her.* **LADY FANNY** *then grabs them from* **CECILY**-*the flowers are ruined by the end.*

To maintain the atmosphere, **SIR THOMAS** *should not be present at the curtain call. Nor, for that matter, should* **MARCUS***, who could possibly arrive late carrying his car keys. An alternative is to have* **SIR THOMAS** *and* **MARCUS** *take very quick bows, in their coats, before dashing out. In this instance,* **SIR THOMAS** *should be constantly talking on the mobile phone.*

CINDERELLA

CINDERELLA

By Michael Green

CINDERELLA, a young girl
SAMMY, a cat
CYSTITIS, Cinderella's ugly sister
HERNIA, another ugly sister
BUTTONS, a cheerful young man, friend to Cinderella
A YOUNG LADY TRUMPETER
PRINCE CHARMING, a young prince
GOOD FAIRY
PROMPTER

And a hand coming round the scenery

PRODUCTION NOTES

Pantomime is a traditional English type of entertainment and if anyone outside of the country should find this piece incomprehensible, I'd understand and advise them to replace it with a play from one of the other volumes.

However, as English readers know only too well, pantomime is all about tradition and this needs to be mirrored in the production. We need all the traditional clichés, such as Cinders leaning on her broom, Buttons leaping around, the life and soul of the party, the principal boy all fishnet tights and thighs. There's an air of desperate jollity about the whole thing, which contrasts with the ineptitude of the production. A pity because they'd always wanted to put on a panto. However, they were sure nobody noticed what went wrong and their friends all said how good it was. It might help the cast to keep this imaginary company in mind as it will aid their own performances. Perhaps they might think of a defective village hall production. Below I sketch out some suggestions on performances, but obviously the cast may adapt these to suit themselves.

The prompt is one of the most important characters and should be played by an actress rather than a prompter. She is totally oblivious to the havoc she has created. The reactions of the cast to her are important. They try to struggle on but exasperation shows.

Buttons is convinced he is the funniest thing on earth. It might be an idea if he tried to do it in Yorkshire but keeps wobbling and going into Irish or Welsh (as one does). He has obviously added dialect lines to the script such as "Ee bah gum" and "deed to goodness". The rest of the cast hate him. Cinderella tries rather too hard to be sweet and finishes up being sugary. Perhaps she puts on a squeaky voice. However, her real nature sometimes breaks out.

Prince Charming (who is, of course, traditionally played by a woman) is about twenty years too old for the part and rather too plump. Her fishnet tights have holes in them. Occasionally she gets her fingernails caught when she slaps her thigh. She tries for a strident principal boy voice but merely deafens everybody. Her local accent might well show through (Welsh?).

The ugly sisters may be played by women or men as preferred. Traditionally, they are usually played by men, but I see no reason why two women shouldn't be cast. They need to be loud-mouthed and distinctly unfeminine. Perhaps posh ladies trying to sound common.

The good fairy is quite wrong for the part. Anyone less graceful couldn't be imagined. I've described her in the text as squat but the main thing is to be awkward and un-fairy-like. She could be huge. Further, she might have a strong regional accent, something completely out of key such as Birmingham, West Country, or Australian.

The flying (or rather non-flying) of the Fairy is vitally important. If the fairy can be flown properly she should descend and ascend jerkily on a ridiculously thick rope. Imagination will suggest what disasters may happen. Alternatively (and more practically) she is meant to be flown but something has gone wrong. ("I told them not to leave it until the dress rehearsal.") So she has to walk on and off with a thick rope attached to her back, trying to give the impression she is floating and waving her wand. The rope can run through a pulley over the stage and another offstage to give the impression they meant to fly her. It might jerk sometimes, as if they were trying to lift her, or it might stop her suddenly. If this results in a rope hanging diagonally from above the stage to the fairy in the wings, have the pulley close to the side where the fairy enters. However, strange ropes dangling about are nothing new in Coarse Theatre.

Sammy the cat rather resents having to be an animal after she read for Cinderella. She thinks it's an easy part so she keeps dropping out of character and behaving like a human, sitting in a chair with crossed legs etc. as indicated in the script. Then she suddenly remembers and goes back into cat mode. Ideally, she should have a proper cat's costume, but it might be possible to improvise or use a mask. The part can also be played by a man.

The herald doesn't often get parts and she is really trying. Perhaps her first show. She's very nervous. It's not her fault the sound operator had one too many in the bar. She realises he is destroying her big chance.

Michael Green

Scene One

CINDERELLA*'s home. The kitchen.*

If necessary, the scene can be set in drapes, with just one flat containing every pantomime cliché—strings of onions hanging down, pots and pans plus a besom broom all painted on the flat. There is a fire in front of the flat, with a genuine flicker effect, and an old-fashioned table and some chairs. If facilities permit, the more flats the better.

When the curtain opens, CINDERELLA *is dusting. She is dressed in the traditional rags.*

Her cat, SAMMY, *sits by the fire. This part can be played by either a man or a woman, but whichever it is, they regret volunteering, because now the cat costume has actually arrived, it is very uncomfortable and keeping up a cat-like stance is tough on the knees. So sometimes* SAMMY *lapses into human poses, scratches the armpits or stands upright.*

CINDERELLA Oh dear. I shall never finish all this work. My two sisters are out enjoying themselves and I have to do all the housework, the sweeping, the dusting, the cooking. It's a shame, isn't it, Sammy?

SAMMY *gives a highly unconvincing miaow.*

And now the fire is going out.

She picks up a log and rather hurriedly thrusts it on top of the fake fire, which promptly explodes. SAMMY *stops being a cat and leaps four feet in the air.*

But you never desert me, do you, Sammy?

The cat shakes its head and miaows again. As
CINDERELLA *dusts, it tries to follow her, but has difficulty*
in walking like a cat. ("I couldn't remember whether the
left leg at the back goes with the right leg at the front,
or if it's left leg and left leg.") **CINDERELLA** *strokes the*
cat and it leans against her leg rather unsteadily, as it
hasn't got used to balancing when crouching. When she
moves away, it falls over.

The door bursts open and the two ugly sisters, **CYSTITIS**
and **HERNIA,** *enter. They are dressed traditionally, like*
washerwomen with striped woollen stockings.

CYSTITIS Oh, me legs is killing me. Take these parcels, Cinderella.

HERNIA And hold these dresses, Cinderella. Go away, cat!

The cat is pestering her. Unfortunately it can't go away
as she is standing on its tail. It makes frantic efforts to
move without success.

CYSTITIS You lazy thing, Cinderella, you haven't cleaned the
floor.

CINDERELLA Yes, Hernia. Yes, Cystitis.

HERNIA Isn't this underwear lovely? *(She holds up a pair of*
red Directoire knickers from a parcel)

CINDERELLA Yes, Hernia.

The cat, now desperate, has slipped out of character
and is tapping **HERNIA's** *leg and pointing to its tail.*
She merely tries to brush it away.

CYSTITIS And isn't this bra divine? *(She holds up something*
like a couple of potato sacks)

CINDERELLA Yes, Cystitis.

HERNIA And where's dinner, Cinderella? Why isn't it ready
for us?

CINDERELLA I've been too busy cleaning, Hernia.

At last **HERNIA** *moves a little and releases the cat, which gives an audible sigh of relief.*

HERNIA Then get it ready at once, you naughty, worthless baggage. Where's that broom? I'm going to spank you.

CINDERELLA By the fireplace, Hernia.

HERNIA *storms across to find the besom broom is painted on the flat. ("Well, you never told me you wanted a real broom, mate.") A pause. She returns empty-handed.*

HERNIA Ah...well...yes...bend over and take that, you naughty girl, and that and that. *(She mimes spanking)*

CINDERELLA Ow, ow. You're hurting.

CYSTITIS I should think she is, you lazy little thing.

A stage management hand comes round the scenery and offers **HERNIA** *a modern broom (the one they use to sweep the stage). She doesn't see it, although the broom is waved vigorously. Eventually, the hand gets fed up and withdraws. It returns immediately and makes a rude sign ("After all the trouble I went to, the silly cow just stood there.").*

HERNIA And now I'm going upstairs to rest. I'm fair worn out.

CYSTITIS Yes, we haven't time to mope around the kitchen all day like our young sister.

The **UGLY SISTERS** *exit.*

CINDERELLA *heaves a sigh.*

CINDERELLA I'd better get on with getting the dinner and start the sweeping or I'll never finish.

CINDERELLA *goes over to the fireplace, only to find the broom is painted on the flat, as did her sister. She stands puzzled.*

A hand again appears round the fireplace flat and offers her a modern broom. She doesn't notice at first, so the broom is banged on the floor twice. Seeing it, she automatically accepts. Then she starts to sweep. After a few strokes, she leaves the broom propped against the fireplace flat and sits on a stool, with a sigh. A hand comes out and snatches the broom back ("Well, we needed it urgently backstage.")

BUTTONS *enters. He is dressed in a traditional pageboy uniform. He obviously fancies himself as the chief comic, although in fact he is totally unfunny. Furthermore, his trousers are dramatically undone, with a strip of shirt sticking out obscenely, a fact of which he is oblivious. He also does not realise that he has a coat hanger dangling from his jacket collar, with a piece of paper on it saying "*BUTTONS*" or "Take in waist". He has decided to play the part in a Northern accent but this keeps slipping into Irish, Welsh, Scots or anything, sometimes in mid-speech.*

BUTTONS *(with ghastly cheeriness)* 'Ullo, 'ullo, 'ullo. How are we today, then? How's me luvly Cinderella, ha, ha, ha, ee bah gum.

CINDERELLA *(not very impressed)* Oh Buttons, how lovely to see you. Your merry voice gladdens my heart. *(She goes to give him a hug and realises his trousers are undone and contents herself with a peck on the cheek)* Oh Buttons, I do like you so very much. *(She points delicately at his crotch)* And I think you like me. *(She points again)*

BUTTONS *(oblivious)* I like you too, Cinders, better than anybody else I know.

CINDERELLA You're the only friend I have in the world. *(She points at his loins, less delicately this time)*

BUTTONS And you're the only friend I have in the world, too, Cinders, except for Sammy the cat. *(He goes over and strokes* **SAMMY***)*

The cat, which has not been paying attention, hastily gets into cat mode.

CINDERELLA Buttons… *(This isn't in the script but she is trying to draw attention to his trousers)*

BUTTONS *(a bit surprised)* Yes, Cinders?

CINDERELLA Nothing, Buttons. Just buttons, Buttons. *(She points at his loins viciously)* Buttons! Buttons!

He remains oblivious, Coarse Actor that he is. But the ad-lib has thrown him. He pauses, waits for a prompt.

BUTTONS *(calling offstage)* Line.

The **PROMPT** *appears, in view of the audience. The* **PROMPT** *is a rather earnest lady in spectacles.*

PROMPT And.

BUTTONS *(sotto voce, as irritated, he moves nearer the* **PROMPT**) And what?

The **PROMPT** *turns the page.*

PROMPT And the.

BUTTONS And the what?

PROMPT No, wrong. You don't say "what".

He glares helplessly. **CINDERELLA** *points to the cat.*

BUTTONS Ah yes, and the cat, the cat, yes, and the cat likes you too, Cinderella.

PROMPT Nearly right.

The **PROMPT** *withdraws.*

CINDERELLA Poor little—

She is interrupted by the return of the **PROMPT**.

PROMPT *(to* **BUTTONS**) You only say "cat" once.

CINDERELLA Poor little Sammy loves everyone, don't you, Sammy?

The cat nods and rubs itself against her. It pats her buttocks with his paw.

I shall never stop loving you, Sammy, you're my only comfort when my sisters bully me. *(Under her breath)* Piss off! *(She removes the offending paw)*

BUTTONS Cinderella, I came to tell you some important news. You know what big balls the king has... *(He fades away and dries, and looks hopefully off stage)*

The **PROMPT** *appears.*

PROMPT Wrong.

The **PROMPT** *withdraws.*

BUTTONS *looks for inspiration to* **CINDERELLA**. *She mimes throwing.*

BUTTONS *(getting it after a moment)* What–er–big dances the king has thrown in the past.

The **PROMPT** *appears.*

PROMPT Balls.

The **PROMPT** *withdraws.*

BUTTONS *(fiercely)* And balls to you. Yes, well, now he's going to throw a bigger ball than ever. It's to be the world's biggest and he's inviting all the nobility and their friends. And what do you think?

CINDERELLA Yes?

BUTTONS Because your poor dead father was Baron Hardup, you and your sisters will qualify for an invitation.

CINDERELLA Me? Go to a ball? I don't believe it.

BUTTONS Yes, you shall go to the ball. Listen!

Silence.

Yes, you shall go to the ball. Listen.

There is a pause.

A voice offstage whispers loudly "Do I go on now?" and rather late a female **HERALD** *enters. She comes on suddenly, having been propelled by a hand in her back. She has a long, cardboard trumpet. It is her first part and she is terrified. The* **HERALD** *raises the trumpet to her lips, glances at the sound operator in his box and blows vigorously. Silence. She tries again. Silence. So she puts her trumpet on her hip in the approved style and starts to say her line.*

HERALD Hear ye, hear—

She is interrupted by the sound of a trumpet. She hastily stops and puts the trumpet to her lips. The call appears to finish. She puts the trumpet at rest again and starts to speak.

Hear ye—

She is again interrupted by a few notes left over from the fanfare. She looks wearily at the sound operator and carries on.

Hear ye, hear ye. Be it known that his majesty invites all citizens of rank to a ball at the palace tomorrow night and you are to receive your invitations in person from the Prince Charming.

PRINCE CHARMING *enters. The* **PRINCE** *is played by a lady of over-generous proportions who is perhaps rather old for the part. However, she is dressed in traditional costume, including black tights.*

The **HERALD** *moves as the* **PRINCE** *enters and treads on the end of her enormous cloak.*

PRINCE *(advancing)* Greetings to everybody in— *(She falls back, clutching her throat, with a strangled shout. After a moment, she recovers. Hoarsely)* Greetings to everybody in this house.

CINDERELLA Greetings, your royal highness.

BUTTONS Likewise, your HRH.

They bow. PRINCE bows back so flamboyantly that she ricks her back. A spasm of pain crosses her face and she gasps. She puts a hand on the injury and gets upright with difficulty.

PRINCE Is this the house of the late Baron Hardup?

CINDERELLA Yes, your royal highness. My name is Cinderella.

PRINCE *(limping downstage with her hand on her back, slapping her thigh and wincing)* What a pretty girl that is. I would like to see more of her.

BUTTONS *(loudly)* I bet you would. And I know which bit you'd like to see. Och ay the noo.

CINDERELLA Now, Buttons.

BUTTONS Now? Don't show him now, wait a bit. Ha, ha, ha. Bah gum and deed to goodness. *(He laughs immoderately)*

The others glare hatred at him ("Talk about overdoing it.").

PRINCE *(savagely)* Oh Buttons dear, no more, please, or I shall die laughing. *(Nothing is less likely judging by her expression)* But to business. I have brought with me tickets for my grand ball at the palace.

BUTTONS I don't want one.

PRINCE Why not?

BUTTONS My face is my ticket. Ha, ha, ha. *(He goes on endlessly)*

PRINCE I have orders to punch all tickets. Ha, ha, ha. *(This is revenge time for the* **PRINCE.** *With a merry laugh, she savagely punches* **BUTTONS** *in the lower part of his stomach)*

BUTTONS *doubles up with a cry of distress. The debate about whether this was deliberate or not will go on for several weeks.*

The **UGLY SISTERS** *burst in.*

CYSTITIS What's all this about a ball at the palace? Can we come?

HERNIA You can't hold it without us. Please, please.

PRINCE Here are invitations for all three of you.

CYSTITIS All three of us? How kind of you to invite Buttons.

PRINCE No, not Buttons, your sister Cinderella.

CYSTITIS Cinderella! You can't invite her.

HERNIA No, she's lazy and idle and sits doing nothing at home all day.

CYSTITIS Besides, she doesn't know how to behave.

HERNIA And she hasn't got anything to wear.

PRINCE *(handing out invitation cards)* None of this matters. I want you all to come and *(to* **CINDERELLA***)* especially you. Please try, Cinderella. *(She retires to the door)* Goodbye everybody. Until we meet at the ball. *(She forgets the injury and bows deeply, which brings forth another gasp of pain)*

The **PRINCE** *exits bent double.*

The **HERALD** *puts the trumpet to her lips, but no sound comes forth, so she doesn't waste time, but shuts the door behind her.*

CINDERELLA What a lovely gentleman—

She is interrupted by the sound of the **HERALD**'s *fanfare ("I thought you'd altered that bit.").*

What a lovely gentleman the prince is.

BUTTONS *(dubiously)* Ay. Lovely. Reet grand. *(Under his breath)* Bitch. *(He feels his bruise)*

CYSTITIS Don't think you're going to the ball, Cinderella. Give us that ticket at once.

CINDERELLA No, I won't, I won't. *(She clutches it to her)*

HERNIA Come along, you stupid girl, give it to us.

CINDERELLA No, no. You shan't have it, you shan't.

They advance upon her. Pussy intervenes to protect her.

SAMMY *(barking threateningly)* Wuff! Wuff! Yap! Yap! *(She growls)*

The **PROMPT** *appears round scenery.*

PROMPT Wrong.

The **PROMPT** *disappears.*

SAMMY *(hastily)* Miaow...miaow. *(She squawks and spits desperately to make up for the lapse of concentration)*

BUTTONS And I'll defend her, too. Bah gum and begorra she shall go to t'ball. Hoots woman awa' w'ye.

HERNIA Oh yes, she won't.

BUTTONS Oh no, she will.

The **PROMPT** *appears.*

PROMPT Wrong.

The **PROMPT** *disappears.*

HERNIA All right, oh no, she won't.

BUTTONS *(to the audience)* Come on, everybody. Support me. Now all together—one, two, three—OH YES, SHE WILL.

The **PROMPT** *peers round the scenery.*

PROMPT *(to the audience)* Right.

The **PROMPT** *disappears.*

HERNIA Never mind, sister, let her keep the invitation. She still won't be able to go because she hasn't anything decent to wear.

CYSTITIS That's right, Hernia, they won't let her in wearing those rags. Keep your ticket, Cinderella, and much good may it do you. Come along, sister, let's look out our best dresses.

As the **UGLY SISTERS** *are going,* **CYSTITIS** *notices* **BUTTON**'s *trousers gaping wide, nudges him, points to the offending place and tugs the coat hanger on his back.*

The **UGLY SISTERS** *exit.*

BUTTONS *looks down, gives a start, and retires with his back to the audience and starts fiddling with his garments. He tears off the coat hanger but the trouser zip sticks. We know because we see his arm jerking.*

CINDERELLA Oh, thank you, Buttons, you were wonderful. Come here and let me give you a kiss.

BUTTONS *is still us fiddling, but he has to say the line.*

BUTTONS Er–yeah, Cinderella, don't worry, it were nowt, ha, ha, ha, baht 'at and bejabbers. *(After a pause he decides to say the line)* Gosh, what a lovely kiss. I do like you Cinderella. Give us another. *(He is still upstage, nowhere near her, tugging at his zip)*

CINDERELLA *(smacking her lips at nothing)* Mmm. I know, Buttons, let's sing a song to cheer us up.

BUTTONS A splendid idea, Cinderella. *(He is still struggling with the zip and ad libs to cover up)* I like a song...ay, a song's a gradely idea...a song...just the job a song is...

Ah! *(At last the zip unsticks suddenly. He gives a cry of pain which suggests it has caught something sensitive. He turns and comes to* CINDERELLA *with a walk indicating injury in the nether regions. He speaks as if in pain)* Yes, I've got a lovely song for us. It's a little ditty that goes like this. *(He sings to the tune of* **"DAISY, DAISY, GIVE ME YOUR ANSWER DO"***)*
CINDERS, CINDERS, HOW WILL YOU GO TO THE BALL?
YOU HAVE NOTHING, NOTHING TO ANSWER THE CALL.
IT WON'T BE SOMETHING FROM GUCCI,
PERHAPS M AND S IF LUCKY.
BUT YOU'LL LOOK SWEET
OH FIT TO EAT
IF YOU WEAR JUST NOTHING AT ALL.

CINDERELLA Oh, that's lovely, Buttons. But it was a bit naughty. Can I sing it with you?

BUTTONS I know, perhaps all these ladies and gentlemen out in the audience would like to join in. You would, wouldn't you?

He appeals to the audience who hopefully answer "Yes". It might be fun to put in a few stooges who shout "No". Whatever the answer, Button's reply is the same.

Good. I knew you would. A right gradely lot isn't it look you.

CINDERELLA But they won't know the words, Buttons.

BUTTONS Oh, I've thought of that. *(He points upwards)*

A song sheet descends from the flies. It is upside down. BUTTONS *notices nothing.*

(with ghastly cheerfulness) Come on, everybody, I really want to hear you. Are you ready? All together now, "Cinders, Cinders..." *(He points at the sheet)*

CINDERELLA *stops him immediately.*

CINDERELLA Buttons.

BUTTONS *stops his song and looks at his trousers.*

BUTTONS *(whispering)* No, I did them up.

CINDERELLA shakes her head and indicates the song sheet. BUTTONS realises what has happened. There is an awkward pause.

Ah...urn...er...yes, well, everybody, that was splendid. The best singing we've had all week. *(He gestures frantically to the stage manager to take up the song sheet)*

Instead of rising, it crashes to the ground, hopefully on BUTTONS. After a short pause, it zooms upwards.

CINDERELLA That was a lovely song, Buttons. It has cheered me up.

A ball of wool suddenly rolls across the stage. It belongs to the PROMPT, who has been knitting.

After a futile attempt to pull it in, the prompt crawls in on hands and knees and retrieves it.

PROMPT So sorry. It slipped, you see.

The PROMPT crawls out.

BUTTONS Well, I must be going. Keep your chin up, Cinderella. Something will turn up, you just wait and see. Goodbye.

CINDERELLA Goodbye, Buttons dear.

They go to kiss. As they do so, the song sheet descends. (It will probably be necessary to use two sheets) This time it is the right way up, if tardy ("You blooming actors are never satisfied...").

BUTTONS *exits disgustedly.*

(trying to navigate the sheet and looking sadly at her invitation) An invitation's no use if I've got nothing to wear, is it, Sammy?

SAMMY, *who has been snoozing at the back, wakes up and reacts by yawning and stretching like a human and putting her paw in front of her mouth.*

SAMMY *(forgetting she is a cat)* No, it isn't. *(She suddenly realises)* Er...miaow...miaow...miaow... *(She frantically tries to redeem herself)*

CINDERELLA I've only got a short time to get a dress and there isn't a hope. I'll just have to write it off as another broken dream. *(She strokes Sammy and softly hums to herself)*

SAMMY *is scratching the armpits, or even the loins.*

Soft music. Slow fade.

Scene Two

The same, some days later.

The lights come up on the scene almost immediately and too quickly for **SAMMY**, *who has unzipped herself so she can scratch better.*

They hastily return to normal. In a vase on the table is a rose. The song sheet is still in position. During **CINDERELLA**'s *first speech it jerkily moves upwards but never properly disappears and remains hanging lopsidedly partly in view. Occasionally, it jerks around as they try to get it up.*

CINDERELLA Oh Sammy, tonight's the night of the Ball and I still haven't got anything to wear. I'll just have to stay at home. And my sisters are so excited.

UGLY SISTERS *enter, in appalling ball gowns.* **HERNIA** *sports a suspiciously large bust.*

CYSTITIS How do I look, Cinderella? Have you ever seen anything so ravishing?

CINDERELLA Never, Cystitis.

HERNIA And what about me, Cinderella. Aren't I even more beautiful?

CINDERELLA Yes, Hernia.

CYSTITIS No, she's not, she can't be more beautiful than me.

A pause. It is **HERNIA**'s *line but she is admiring herself in a mirror.*

PROMPT Oh, yes, l can.

HERNIA *(angrily)* All right. Oh, yes, I can.

CYSTITIS Oh, no, you can't.

HERNIA Oh, look at the lovely rose. I must pin it on my dress. *(She goes to the table, takes the flower, and looks in her dress for a pin. There isn't one. She looks at the others)*

Suddenly the **PROMPT***'s hand comes out, holding a large hatpin.* **HERNIA** *gratefully seizes it and pins the rose to her bosom. Unfortunately, the bosom consists mainly of a balloon which explodes. There is a ghastly pause.*

CYSTITIS *(bravely)* Come along, hurry up, we'll be late, sister.

HERNIA *(picking bits of rubber out of her bosom)* Yes, all right, sister. Don't wait up, Cinderella, we may be late. What a pity you hadn't anything to wear.

CYSTITIS Just as well, I'd say. She'd only disgrace us. Come along, can't you?

The **UGLY SISTERS** *exit.*

The song sheet jerks frantically and at last vanishes. Pause. It then reappears suddenly, dangling by one rope.

CINDERELLA *sighs and goes to the fireplace for the broom, but she didn't see it being removed by a mysterious hand in the previous scene. She stands nonplussed for a moment and then a besom broom is pushed on stage by a modern broom. The modern broom knocks twice on the floor to attract her attention. She turns and sees it and picks up the besom. She sweeps a little and then rests on the broom handle in the traditional Cinders' position.*

CINDERELLA Oh Sammy, I'm so unhappy.

The broom snaps, throwing her to the floor.

There is a sudden flash on one side of the stage and after a short delay, the **GOOD FAIRY** *appears on the other side. Unlike most* **GOOD FAIRIES***, she is squat, fat and malevolent. Attached to her back is a thick rope by which* *she is supposed to be flown from a pulley above the stage, but something has gone wrong and she remains earthbound, although flapping her arms hopefully (see production notes).*

Who are you?

FAIRY I am your good fairy godmother.

CINDERELLA I didn't think I'd got one.

FAIRY Oh yes, you have. Everybody has a Fairy Godmother.

CINDERELLA I don't believe in fairies.

The PROMPT *appears.*

PROMPT Wrong play.

The PROMPT *disappears.*

FAIRY Oh, yes, you do.

The PROMPT *appears.*

PROMPT Sorry, I thought you'd slipped into Peter Pan. Sorry. Sorry.

The PROMPT *vanishes and re-appears immediately.*

We did it last year, you see. Sorry.

The PROMPT *disappears.*

CINDERELLA Well, I suppose I must. Why are you here?

FAIRY Cinderella, would you like to go to the ball?

CINDERELLA Oh yes, I'd love to, but I haven't anything to wear.

FAIRY Would you go if you had a lovely dress to wear like all the other ladies?

CINDERELLA Oh yes, oh yes, I would, I would. *(She moves to the side of the stage where the flash is)*

FAIRY Then, Cinderella, you shall go to the ball.

CINDERELLA *waits expectantly. The* FAIRY *waves her wand madly. Nothing happens. The* FAIRY *tries again.*

(shouting) Cinderella, you shall...

The flash goes off unexpectedly, catching both unawares.

CINDERELLA *runs off.*

...go to the ball. Now to bring her back transformed into a beautiful lady. One...two...three... Hey presto! *(She waves her wand for the second flash and* CINDERELLA*'s return. Nothing happens as* CINDERELLA *isn't ready. Nonplussed, she carries on counting)* Four...five...six...seven. Hey presto! *(She waves her wand again. Nothing happens)* Eight...nine... ten...eleven...

The flash goes off suddenly, but CINDERELLA *is late and doesn't come on behind it. Raised voices indicate a struggle offstage.*

CINDERELLA *rushes on afterwards in great haste. The quick change has obviously been too much for her. She has a magnificent blonde wig with two long pigtails but it is on backwards. So is the splendid ball gown she now wears. Consequently, it is only half done up and at the front, too.*

CINDERELLA *stares wildly at the* FAIRY, *who goggles back.*

(weakly) Hey presto...

CINDERELLA Oh, I can't believe it. Look at me!

FAIRY You are beautiful, Cinderella. You will be the ball of the belle.

CINDERELLA Oh, I feel so happy...

The PROMPT *appears.*

PROMPT No. Ding-dong.

The **PROMPT** *disappears.*

FAIRY *(savagely)* I mean the belle of the bell...the ball of the...
you'll look lovely...

CINDERELLA *(patience wearing thin)* Oh, I feel so happy, I
could dance all night.

FAIRY So you shall, Cinderella.

CINDERELLA But wait a moment. How am I going to get to the
palace? I can't walk through the streets in this lovely gown.

FAIRY Don't worry, I've thought of that, Cinderella. Just look
outside through the window. *(There is no window, a fact
which dawns on her)* I mean the...er...fireplace.

CINDERELLA A coach and four! Is that for me? And footmen
as well!

FAIRY Now remember, Cinderella. You must not tell anybody
who you are. And my spell ends at midnight. Then you will
return to your normal self. Everything will vanish–your fine
clothes, footmen, the coach. Be home by twelve or else...
And now farewell! I must fly back to Fairyland to have
supper with the elves. *(She now prepares to fly away. She
looks expectantly into the wings and then up into the flies,
and holds her arms out like wings. She holds this pose for
several seconds but nothing happens. To help matters, she
jumps up and down a few times, flapping)*

*The large rope at her back twitches vainly. Faint cries
of "Heave" may be heard. After several futile attempts
she gives up and makes for the exit sulkily.*

(flapping her arms) Farewell, Cinderella. Upwards I fly,
ever upwards to the stars. Farewell...

The **FAIRY** *exits.*

CINDERELLA *(looking upwards)* Goodbye, Fairy Godmother.
And now for my coach and off to the palace for the ball!

CINDERELLA *runs out.*

Slow fade. As the lights fade, the music of the ball gradually rises. A traverse curtain is drawn across the stage, hiding the kitchen and the next scene is played in front of it.

Scene Three

This is played in front of the traverse.

The ball. Sounds of music and jollity.

The UGLY SISTERS *enter.*

CYSTITIS I don't think I'm enjoying this ball very much. Nobody seems to want to dance.

HERNIA I've never seen such a terrible lot of people.

CYSTITIS *(looking offstage)* What's that?

HERNIA What's what?

CYSTITIS It's a man!

HERNIA Ah!

The UGLY SISTERS *exit rapidly in pursuit of him.*

CINDERELLA, *who is masked, and the* PRINCE, *come in from the other side. The* PRINCE *is upright, if limping.*

PRINCE You are easily the prettiest girl at the ball. And that dress. It is positively ravishing!

It is still backwards.

And your hair!

CINDERELLA *tried to correct her wig in a hurry in the wings, with the result it is now sideways.*

CINDERELLA Your Highness is too kind. And how good of you to escort me all evening.

PRINCE I was struck by your beauty as soon as you entered the bathroom–er–ballroom. Let's dance again. May I have the honour?

CINDERELLA curtsies and the PRINCE bows magnificently. Alas, once more she overdoes it and her back gives way. She clutches CINDERELLA as best she can and tries to dance with one hand on her back.

I'm sure we've met somewhere before. There's something about you that is familiar. And why do you wear that mask? Why won't you tell me your name?

CINDERELLA I mustn't.

PRINCE Why not?

CINDERELLA It's a secret. Aaaaahhhh.

The exclamation is wrung from her as the PRINCE is hit by a spasm and clings to her for support.

Chimes are heard.

PRINCE Ah, midnight. Time for supper.

CINDERELLA Midnight! Already! Are you sure?

PRINCE Just count them. Five–six–seven–eight–nine–ten–eleven...

An awkward pause. Number twelve doesn't come, so she presses on without it.

Must you go so soon?

CINDERELLA Yes, I...

The missing chime sounds.

Yes, I must.

A thirteenth chime sounds.

Please remember me. Goodbye, goodbye.

CINDERELLA runs off trying to shed a slipper. It won't come off despite her savage kicking. Eventually she exits, removes it in the wings, and throws it back at the PRINCE. Hopefully it hits her in the face.

PRINCE Hullo, someone's dropped a slipper. *(She goes to pick it up but gives a shriek of pain and leaves it)* It must belong to that pretty girl who wouldn't tell me her name. I must see her again. Tomorrow I shall go through all the city to find whose foot fits this slipper and when I find her, she shall be my bride and live at the palace. *(She makes a tentative effort to pick up the slipper, gives up, and kicks it offstage)*

Blackout—rather early for the **PRINCE** *who is stranded in darkness.*

Scene Four

The traverse is drawn back, revealing the kitchen.

*Lights up, showing the **PRINCE** groping her way off and moaning.*

***SAMMY** is caught sitting in a chair with legs crossed like a human and puffing a lighted cigarette. Surprised, she starts coughing badly and coughs round the stage, trying to dispose of the cigarette. She stubs it out on a loaf of bread and hastily resumes cat mode.*

***UGLY SISTERS** enter, still in ball gowns.*

CYSTITIS I love this dress so much I'm never going to take it off.

HERNIA I slept in mine.

CYSTITIS I had a bath in mine. *(She accidentally treads on **SAMMY**'s foot)*

***SAMMY** loses all traces of being a cat and hops around the room on one leg, holding the toe and shouting and swearing.*

SAMMY Oh God, my toe. Ah, it's agony. Oh, sod me! Aaaah! *(She tries to kick **CYSTITIS**)*

HERNIA Where's that lazy girl, Cinderella?

CYSTITIS She's not down yet. I'll give her what for. Cinderella! Come down this instant and make breakfast.

***SAMMY** lands a kick.*

Aah!

CINDERELLA *(offstage)* Coming.

HERNIA Lazy baggage!

***CINDERELLA** enters. She hasn't had time to make her quick change, so she's in ball gown with rags on top.*

CINDERELLA I'm sorry, I overslept.

CYSTITIS Overslept indeed! And you didn't even go to the Ball.

A knock on the door. The **HERALD** *enters, bearing a cushion with a slipper on it. She is followed by the* **PRINCE**, *who now leans heavily on a walking stick.*

HERALD Know ye—

Although this time she doesn't even have a trumpet, she is interrupted by a brief trumpet blast, which stops suddenly.

Know ye that His Royal Highness wishes to find the owner of this beautiful glass slipper left at the ball last night and any lady whom the slipper fits shall be his bride and shall reign with him at the palace.

CYSTITIS Be his bride! Come on, let's try it on. *(She tries on the slipper)*

The slipper is not the one **CINDERELLA** *dropped, but a special one produced by the props department to look like glass. It is a monstrosity, probably made out of canvas and painted silver ("Well, it's difficult to make it look like glass, mate.") However, it fits* **CYSTITIS** *perfectly.*

Oh, it's agony! Such a shame. I'm sure the prince could love me.

HERNIA Let me try.

Once again the slipper fits perfectly.

Oh dear, it won't fit me either.

HERALD What about the other lady?

CYSTITIS Oh you needn't bother about her.

HERALD Come along, madam.

CINDERELLA tries the slipper on. It causes her agony but she pretends it's a perfect fit.

CINDERELLA *(limping about in great pain)* It fits admirably.

PRINCE So it was you who I fell in love with at the ball! I might have guessed it. Come back to the palace with me and we shall be married tomorrow.

CINDERELLA My prince! *(She goes to embrace her but the stick is in the way and she accidentally kicks it away)*

The **PRINCE** *sags and groans.*

Can I take Sammy?

PRINCE Of course you can.

> **SAMMY** *stands up and shakes her hand and then remembers she's a cat and drops down miaowing. There is a flash.*

> *The* **GOOD FAIRY** *enters, on the end of a rope as before.*

FAIRY And so Prince Charming married the kitchen girl Cinderella the very next day, and they all lived happily ever after.

> *As before, she signals for her hoist but it fails to come. As she is vainly jumping up and down, the cast say the final lines.*

PRINCE *(looking up)* Goodbye, little fairy.

CINDERELLA *(looking up)* Goodbye, Fairy Godmother. You were a real godmother to me. Goodbye. *(She waves at the flies)*

> **ALL** *cast look up.*

ALL Goodbye.

FAIRY Bollocks.

> *The* **FAIRY** *is still jumping up and down like a ruptured crab and flapping her arms as the lights fade or the curtain falls.*

> *Traditional curtain call.*

During it the **PROMPT** *insists on sticking her head out and waving.*

SAMMY *takes it in human mode, waving to friends in the audience. The* **PRINCE** *forgets her back injury and once more bows deeply with disastrous results.*

The End

TRAPPED

FURNITURE AND PROPERTY LIST

On stage: Built-in cupboard with jammed door
             Small table laid for tea with sandwiches, cutlery,
                tea cups, etc.
             Table or desk with drawer. *On it:* old-fashioned
                phone with loose cord
             Spears and shields and stuffed animal's head on
                walls (perhaps painted)
             Chairs
             Carpet
             Tablecloth
             Vase

Offstage: Briefcase (**Braithwaite**)
             Walking stick (**SM**)
             Spear (**Braithwaite**)
             Revolver (**SM**)
             Script in ring binder (**SM**)

Personal: **Major:** moustache
             George: sword sticking out of waistband
             Sheila: handkerchief
             SM: policeman's helmet, spectacles, books

LIGHTING PLOT

Property fittings required: nil

One interior setting. The same throughout

To open: Overall general lighting

Cue 1   Music   (Page 5)
            Slowly fade lights to blackout,
               then bring them up again.

| Cue 2 | **Sheila:** "And I was his god-daughter." | (Page 9) |
| | *Sudden blackout, then bring lights up when ready.* | |

EFFECTS PLOT

TRAPPED

Cue 1	**House manager:** "Thank you."	(Page 5)
	Dramatic music, perhaps Beethoven's Fifth.	
Cue 2	Lights go down and come up	(Page 5)
	Phone rings, and after a while stops ringing.	
Cue 3	**Maid:** "...isolated old country house in Surrey."	(Page 6)
	Phone rings loudly, continuing.	
Cue 4	**Maid** replaces receiver	(Page 6)
	Cut phone ringing.	
Cue 5	**Maid** picks up receiver	(Page 6)
	Phone rings, stopping after a few rings.	
Cue 6	Major: "That's strange, the door won't open."	(Page 10)
	Sound of thunder, howling wind and storm.	
Cue 7	**Freda** comforts **Sheila**	(Page 11)
	Increase noise of storm.	
Cue 8	**Braithwaite** dies	(Page 16)
	Pistol shot in the wings.	

OEDOCLES, KING OF THEBES

FURNITURE AND PROPERTY LIST

Scene One

On stage: Rostra
Classic column
Stretcher with loosely attached handles, carrying **Ovary** covered with white sheet

Scene Two

On stage: As before

Scene Three

On stage: As before

Offstage: Large garden shears (**Priestess**)

Scene Four

On stage: As before

Offstage: Shears (**Amnesia**)
Plate with two golf balls covered by handkerchief (**Amnesia**)

Scene Five

Set: Small monument topped by 2 stone globes

Offstage: Leafy branches, young tree trunks (**Chorus**)

Personal: **Oedocles:** ghastly grey wig

LIGHTING PLOT

Property fittings required: nil

Two simple settings

Scene One

To open: Overall lighting suggesting heat

Cue 1   **Hysterectomy** and **Chorus** exit   (Page 26)
            Fade lights down slowly.

Scene Two

To open: Overall general lighting

No cues.

Scene Three

To open: Overall general lighting

Cue 2   **Amnesia** exits   (Page 31)
            Instant blackout.

Cue 3   **Oedocles** and **Priestess** fall   (Page 31)
            Bring lights up immediately.

Scene Four

To open: Spot on **Oedocles**

Cue 4   All dribble out   (Page 34)
            Blackout.

Scene Five

To open: Overall general lighting

Cue 5   **Chorus** hurl themselves on **Oedocles**   (Page 40)
            Fade lights down slowly.

EFFECTS PLOT

Cue 1   To open Scene One   (Page 23)
            Taverna music.

PRIDE AT SOUTHANGER PARK

FURNITURE AND PROPERTY LIST

Scene One

On stage:	Chaise-longue. *On it:* fake toy dog
	Armchair
	Table with flowers in vase

Offstage:	Bible (**Reverend**)
	Cigarette (**William**)

Personal:	**Cecily:** watch, fan
	Lady Fanny: fan
	Mrs Squires: fan
	FOH manager: powerful torch
	Reverend: crucifix, mitre (worn throughout)
	Gladys: cap too small for her
	Sir Thomas: padding, huge grey sideburns (worn throughout)

Scene Two

On stage:	As before

Offstage:	Refreshments trolley (**FOH manager**)
	Flowers (**FOH manager**)
	Car keys (optional) (**Marcus**)

Personal:	**Marcus:** heavy sideburns
	Gladys: huge cap
	FOH manager: torch
	Sir Thomas: mobile phone

LIGHTING PLOT

Property fittings required: nil
One interior setting. The same throughout

Scene One

To open: Darkness

Cue 1	Music plays *Bring lights up.*	(Page 47)
Cue 2	Music starts again *Blackout.*	(Page 56)

Scene Two

To open: Overall general lighting

Cue 3	**Reverend:** "...and everlasting light." *Sudden blackout.*	(Page 58)
Cue 4	**Marcus:** "Tell him to get those lights up again." *Bring lights up.*	(Page 58)
Cue 5	**Gladys** moves forward to take her bow *Fade lights down.*	(Page 66)

EFFECTS PLOT

Cue 1	Lights go down *Fuzzy recording of soundtrack from "**GONE WITH THE WIND (TARA'S THEME)**", continuing.*	(Page 35)
Cue 2	**Cecily** turns and runs to **Lady Fanny** *Cut music with a screech.*	(Page 47)
Cue 3	**Cecily:** "But aunt..." *After a pause doorbell rings, electric, preferably with silly tune.*	(Page 49)
Cue 4	**Lady Fanny:** "...with the first of our guests?" *Doorbell rings.*	(Page 49)
Cue 5	**Cecily** stands up and sits down again *Doorbell rings.*	(Page 52)
Cue 6	**Reverend** supports Cecily on way out *Music.*	(Page 56)

Cue 7	To open Scene Two	(Page 57)
	Fade music with hiss and squeak.	

Cue 8	**Sir Thomas:** "...you have lived under	
	our roof..."	(Page 63)
	Sir Thomas's *mobile phone rings.*	

| Cue 9 | **Gladys** moves forward to take her bow | (Page 66) |
| | *Music.* | |

CINDERELLA

FURNITURE AND PROPERTY LIST

Scene Two

On stage: Flat painted with strings of onions hanging down,
pots and pans, besom broom
Fire
Old-fashioned table. *On it:* vase
Chairs
Log of wood
Stool
Song sheet from the flies

Offstage: Parcel containing pair of red Directoire knickers
(**Hernia**)
Parcel containing bra looking like a couple of potato
sacks (**Cystitis**)
Modern broom
Long cardboard trumpet (**Herald**)
Invitation cards (**Prince**)
Ball of wool (**Prompt**)

Personal: **Buttons:** coat hanger with note "Buttons" or "Take
in waist"
Prompt: spectacles (worn throughout)

Scene Two

Set: Rose in vase on table

Offstage:	Large hat pin (**Prompt**)
	Besom broom (pushed on with modern broom)
	Wand (**Good Fairy**)
Personal:	**Hernia:** balloon hidden in bosom
	Good Fairy: thick rope
	Cinderella: blonde wig with two long pigtails

Scene Three

Set:	Traverse
Personal:	**Cinderella:** mask, wig

Scene Four

Strike:	Traverse
Offstage:	Cushion with slipper made of canvas and painted silver (**Herald**)
	Walking stick (**Prince**)
	Lighted cigarette (**Sammy**)
Personal:	**Good Fairy:** thick rope

LIGHTING PLOT

Property fittings required: nil
Two simple interior settings

Scene One

To open: Overall lighting, and flicker effect on fire

Cue 1	**Cinderella** thrusts a log on top of fake fire	(Page 73)
	Explosion effect on fire.	
Cue 2	Soft music plays	(Page 86)
	Fade lights down slowly.	

Scene Two

To open: Bring lights up too quickly

Cue 3	**Cinderella:** "Oh Sammy, I'm so unhappy." *Sudden flash on one side of stage.*	(Page 88)
Cue 4	Good Fairy waves her wand second time *Flash.*	(Page 90)
Cue 5	Good Fairy: "Eight...nine...ten... eleven..." *Sudden flash.*	(Page 90)
Cue 6	Cinderella runs out *Fade lights down slowly.*	(Page 92)

Scene Three

To open: Overall general lighting

Cue 7	**Prince** kicks slipper *Blackout suddenly, too early for* **Prince**.	(Page 94)

Scene Four

To open: Overall general lighting

Cue 8	Sammy shakes hands with Prince, then miaows *Flash.*	(Page 98)
Cue 9	**All:** "Goodbye." *Fade lights down.*	(Page 98)

EFFECTS PLOT

Cue 1	**Cinderella** thrusts log on top of fake fire *Explosion effect.*	(Page 73)
Cue 2	**Herald:** "Hear ye, hear—" *Sound of trumpet interrupting.*	(Page 79)
Cue 3	**Herald:** "Hear ye—"	(Page 79)

*A few notes left over from trumpet
fanfare interrupting.*

THIS
IS
NOT
THE
END

Lightning Source UK Ltd.
Milton Keynes UK
UKHW021953011219
354566UK00005B/154/P